T'S BU

MW00974639

NOT

PERSONAL

----

inally, A Book That Truly Separates The acts About Funding For Your Small Busi-ess. Personal Credit And Business Credit re Similar But Operates Completely Differ-nt. This Book Will Make It Clear.

Author: Robert Wilson

W. A. C.

Wealth Accumulation Concepts

Copyright © 2004 by Wealth Accumulation Concepts

ISBN 0-9721065-1-0

Published in Atlanta, Georgia, by Wealth Accumulation Conc

www.unlockingwealth.com

Printed by Print 1 Direct Marietta, Georgia

Printed in the United States of America

TABLE OF CONTENT

Introduction

That's right, It's Business, Not Personal. You, as an entrepreneur, mus begin to change your outlook in order to change your outcome. Many hard-working entrepreneurs like you have the desire to build the next fortune 500 company. Even if that is not your dream, the work that is quired is the same at start-up.

Often at start-up, the entrepreneur feels that he/she must find the rigl source to get the funding needed to take their business idea to the nex level. In the process, many skip over some of the very basic processes that have made companies successful. In this book, I intend to share some of the many tools that I have found invaluable in achieving my goals.

This will not in any way make you an expert on the subject; however, believe that there is tons of information that comes our way on a daily basis. This information sometimes needs to be interpreted for the layp son. Without having some of this knowledge, you may find it a back-breaking effort to try to decipher it on your own.

One of my goals in this book is to also lay a foundation for many of yo to be able to separate your personal profile from your business profile. liave hcard many stories about how other nationalities have an overall advantage over minorities in the business world. I will make a case th business is business.

With this information I believe the main ingredient in the recipe for su cess will be you. A professor at a local business college once told me th the key element for a successful business is a P.H.D. (Passion, Heart ar Desire). I expect that to be true only after the real work have been don

Entrepreneurs must understand that they and they alone must create their preparedness. That is vital in realizing the full scope of their drea That vision must manifest itself on paper *and* to a plan. A plan that esta lishes readiness and willingness seems to always be present regardless preparedness. Why is this so important? Let's see.

Chapter 1

IT'S NOT PERSONAL

Allow me to share with you my story, *The Broke Millionaire*. Over 10 year ago I had the dream to be my family's first entrepreneur. It started with the idea of a chain of fast food restaurants (Rally's) to be centered right in the middle of the famous triangle in North Carolina. The goal was to place seventy-five burger joints in a twenty-mile area surrounded by almost 100 colleges and technical schools.

The college student budget fit perfectly into the plan - late night fast food, availability near every campus and lots of production. With selected areas identified and researched, my willingness over-took my readiness.

I knew what my dream was and visualized how it would happen but that was not enough. The problem was, there was no readiness. The plan was mostly in my head and not in my heart.

Every single time I went to speak with someone about this awesome opportunity, they always seemed to want a business plan. Not just any business plan would do; they wanted to see the funding plan, a marketing plan, a projection, a financial statement and even a management team. I would look at them and think, "This is their way to hold a brother down".

Regardless of how I addressed their concerns, they still had other questions - questions that indicated they were not inclined to give me the money. It looked to me as if they were deliberately trying to discourage me.

Over and over again, each time I would ask myself, "Why are they blocking this great opportunity?" Can they not see the full vision here? Then one day I set up a meeting with a man named George Andrews.

At the time, George was working very hard to start a venture of his own. His idea was to open a bank; not a national bank, but a local black bank. That day he gave me two hours of his time.

For the first time money was not discussed. What he did give me wa
business readiness lesson which involved telling me why all the othe
potential lenders had asked for the basic steps of how I planned to tal
to achieve my venture.

The lesson still was not learned though. I heard what he said but I di
not understand, nor did I want to at the time. I saw nearly 200,000 st
dents yearly in that area that needed a reasonably priced place to eat.

Then I went to the franchises and pitch them my dream. To my surpr
they all asked for the same things. With that, I gave up. I was willin
but not ready. I was not willing to do what it took, the dirty work of
putting together a plan. "Let someone else do it," I told myself, "I ha
the dream."

A year later I lost my father. After his death, I realize that I must truly
become the first link to building wealth. My father left me only a pair
boots. The very ones he died in.

After four very difficult months that can only be described as life chan
ing, I receive a vision from God. That vision leads me to design a devi
to used for your upper-body fitness called "Rojen". .

This piece of equipment was hot! Now keep in mind that at that time
was not into fitness in that way. I played ball and jogged every now
and then, but that was about it. That's why I knew that this vision wa
directly from the Almighty. I had a great idea and began the work of
developing what the public was asking for.

I did the business plan, marketing plan, financial projection statement
funding plan, and put together a management team. I located a manu
facturer and a research and development company for the project.

I met with Nathaniel Bronner, Jr., a man I respect and admire as a grea
business mind. He immediately got onboard and provided me with
funding for some research and development. This gave me the chance
to work to pull the whole project together.

Once we had some possible designs on paper, it was just a matter of deciding what steps to take next. Nathaniel   discussed how we would go about presenting our product to the market. He told me that he was willing and ready to take to the market, but I rejected his advice because I was determined to do it my way.

Well, years passed and I continued to try to get it done my way. It did not happen. Eventually the product made its way to television and was sold in hundreds of markets as the AB Machine on wheels. You may even have one.

I shared these stories of illusive success despite hard work and effort because I believe we all will have such experiences. The true measure is what we learn from them. My particular problem was two-fold: I lacked readiness and my desire was rooted in selfishness. I hope all of you entrepreneurs will benefit from my mistakes and learn some valuable lessons that will contribute to your success.

See your dream to be a business owner in stages. As you lay your vision out on paper, set stages that will allow you to make the best run at your goal.

In this book, we will explore areas of funding and credit issues. I will refer to business plans and the tools that go along with them. You will find that you need this information. Imagine right now where you are with your business goals.

What would be the first question you ask yourself? What would you think is needed the most? Where are you centered as it relates to making this dream of yours come true? I believe that as you ponder those questions you may find that the business of realizing your vision can seem rather hard at the start.

You're right! It can and will be as hard as you make it. There is another choice for you as well. That choice is to simply do business any way you can. I like the quote " by any means necessary" except when it applies to doing business.

Many small business owners have made doing business a game of Ru
sian roulette. You may very well know people who have built their
business for years and have never attempted to get funding. Yet, in t
business world there were many opportunities that were never taken
advantage of because of a particular mode of operation.

At this point, allow me to say that if you refuse or do not desire to use
any of the information found in this book that's just fine. At least try
clearly see what I am trying to provide to you to go to another level.
is about doing business, right? So do business!

Chapter 2

Specific Requirements of Lenders

Many of you have heard me on my radio show and in seminars talking about personal credit. Most of the fake, so-called credit specialists do not have a real clue about building credit. You are going to hear again some familiar information related to business credit.

Personal credit and business credit share some of the same requirements. These requirements all have variable that set the standard in establishing credit. There is no simple solution such as taking a pill at night and waking up in the morning with credit. Many of you will have some work to do.

It is impossible to provide specific requirements for each type of loan, because of the many variables each lender has. It is also impossible because the lending market changes daily based on the economy and world events.

World event also present the opportunity to create a new business by improving the quality of life. You can assess world events, identify a void that exists in the marketplace and fill a need with your product or idea.

You may be surprised to know what products always sell well when the economy is down. Believe it or not, it's cosmetics and costume jewelry. Think about it; it really is, women who care about keeping up their appearance even though they can't afford luxuries such as salon services or high-end jewelry.

Another consideration that affects the requirements is the amount of money the lender has to grant at the time you apply. Some lenders will be less restrictive if they have not made many loans and have a large amount to lend in a month and more restrictive when the opposite is true.

If you think of it in terms of "Mother's Milk", you'll see what I'm really saying is that if the money is not on hand, it won't be available to you. The concept that the Milk is not always available can sometimes be difficult for the startup business owner to understand.

On the other hand, it really should be simple. You should know what a budget is and if it is not there, it's not there.

Whether you are seeking a loan from an old-line commercial bank, a sophisticated venture capitalist, or an asset-based lender, there are certain essentials that any lender looks for before extending credit. This is the **readiness** that I like to talk about.

There are some areas that many entrepreneurs and small business owners take for granted. The assumption that, "I know where I want my business to go and how I want to run my business" can be the hindrance of any growth. Readiness means getting the requirements in place for the lender.

Basically, all lenders want assurance that their loan will be repaid; collateral is always important- but lenders also want credible evidence that your business venture will be successful. Your job is to put forward a funding proposal that addresses every lender's concerns and accurately reflects your prospects for success.

I will be repeating some important facts in this book for the sole purpose of trying to change your concept of operating a business. There are so many people who have operated their business for years and for the most part have been very successful.

Each year they have earned a profit, seen growth, and even expanded their business. Believe it or not, they have never even considered 5 of the 8 essentials that you will find on the next page.

Now, after you have read them and completely understand them, just imagine the possible growth and expansion that could be realized just by incorporating these essentials into the way you do business. We take things personally and we handle them differently.

"Why is it not the same when we do business? "

Folks, I will continue to say it over and over again **"It's Business Not Personal"** and when you, as an entrepreneur, get that embedded in your head, you're on your way to another level.

Readiness will give you the upper hand. Readiness is the great divide. Take a good look at these essentials and make the adjustments.

The Basics All Lenders Look For

Character - -No lender will part with his or her money unless he or she senses that you are a person of integrity. A good business reputation and a sound credit history count for a lot.

Anyone known for questionable business dealings will have a tough time with any lender-regardless of the venture prospects. Go ahead and create the world's next wonder-business and be known as a shady person. See how much money you get.

Management Capability - Lenders want to know your track record. Whether you are starting a new business or expanding an existing one, any potential creditor will want evidence that you have successfully managed a business in the past and can continue to do so in the future.

Market Share - Is there a substantial market for the product or service you are offering? This is very important for the growth of your business. Be prepared to back up your assertions with solid market research, (surveys, studies, etc.), preferably prepared by independent organizations.

Strategic Plan - All lenders want a road map of where you intend to go with your business, and the strategy that will take you there. A funding proposal with financial forecasts is essential.

Your forecasts must be based on reasonable assumptions, supported by your market research, that indicate sufficient cash flow to repay creditors in accordance with the terms of any financing agreement.

Sound Financials - If you've been in business for more than a year you'll be asked to present financial statements such as income statements and balance sheets that reflect operations in line with industry norms.

Lenders love to look at financial ratios (i.e. debt-to-equity, inventory turnover, and accounts receivable turnover, etc.) to assess your financial health. Can you possibly see how important it is for you to learn to do your financial ratios? There is a real connection between your personal behavior and your business.

If your business doesn't fall within the norms for your industry, (your banker, CPA, or attorney can advise you on this) be prepared to state why. Potential creditors will often check on your personal credit history as well. So it's a good idea to review your own report from a credit-reporting agency and to clear up discrepancies before you approach a lender.

Demonstrated Cash Flow - Every business needs working capital to make it a success, and most lenders want to know that you have sufficient "coverage" - not sweat equity. You will need to be able to show there is cash flow in the business. That is why I will always question showing a financial loss.

That is, they really want to know that you generate cash flow somewhere between 125 percent and 150 percent of what it takes to stay current on their loan after other expenses have been accounted for.

Lenders usually dislike extending credit if they see that a portion of the loan proceeds is allocated to repayment of owner or stockholder loans, or if you are trying to replace another lender who is bowing out.

They also want to know what you have contributed to the venture besides just sweat. If you have real dollars invested in the business, you're at risk too, and that is a plus. Parenthetically, you will probably be required to subordinate your equity or loan investment.

Collateral - Any sophisticated lender asks for security on a loan. The collateral package you are asked to provide may include a pledge of personal assets or a guarantor who is a co-signer with a substantial net worth.

Terms - The best bet is to seek advice from your financial advisor (banker, CPA, attorney, etc.) to get an insight about payback terms your business can expect. It is important to frame the loan application according to the terms the bank can offer.

Other Requirements

A business has the ability to obtain a loan in the business name only, depending on the type of loan, the amount of the loan, the lender, and the time the loan is requested.

Other key elements that lenders look for in businesses to approve a business-only loan are:

- Business Credit Score and Profile
- Age of Business
- Annual Revenue of Business
- Profits of the Business
- Financial Statements
- Tax Returns
- Down-Payment
- Business' Ability to Make Payments
- Does the Business have a Merchant Account?
- Does the Business have Accounts Receivable?
- What is the Value of the Business' Assets?
- Does the Business Have any Equipment, that is lien free?
- Business Plan

Original Quote

Here is a quote to think about before you read about the Mother's Milk.

A journeyman that prepares for a journey not only carries along just supplies such as food, water and clothing. He/she must also consider the opportunities that lie ahead. These opportunities can range from a number of things that may be required to finish the journey.

He/she must also consider and prepare for disaster as well. That will demand that certain types of tools are selected. The tools should be able to repair, build and simply modify if needed. The tools may ultimately end up as being the lifeline to the journey.

The same will be true with your business. Get them and learn to use the tools.

Robert Wilson

Chapter 3

Borrowing Money

You Need Money, Right?

It is often said that small business people have a difficult time borrowing money. This is not necessarily true. Banks make money by lending money. They just do not give money out haphazardly. When I use the term "Mother's Milk," that shows that there is a need, as well as a readiness for the milk.

However, the inexperience of many small business owners in financial matters often prompts banks to deny loan requests. The same is true in any financial process that you will ultimately face.

Requesting a loan when you are not properly prepared sends a signal to your lender. That message is: High Risk! To be successful in obtaining a loan, you must be prepared and organized. I call this having the readiness. You are probably going to be tired of this word before you finish reading the book.

You must know exactly how much money you need, why you need it, and how you will pay it back. You must be able to convince your lender that you are a good credit risk. S.B.A. and the I.R.S. (Small Business Resource Guide) and many other resources are out there to give you help with this process.

Money is the Mother's Milk of business. It fuels the gestation and germination of business ideas; it sustains the launching of a new enterprise; it nurtures the process of growth and development. Start-up businesses devour large sums to buy things, and operating businesses requires substantial sums to keep them going.

Entrepreneurs can't open a store without cash in the till, and they can't run a production plant without money in their checking account. There's no chicken and egg issue here; the money comes first.

Businesses that start on a shoestring are among the most likely to end up strung out. It is sad but true; the money comes first in the funding process. Be not confused; the business plan of the busines must exist.

The Mother's Milk is what makes a baby elephant grow by hundreds of pounds before it is cut lose. There are three things that I really want to reiterate about money and its importance as "The Mother's Milk."

The gestation and germination is the period of growth and devel opment stage of your business concepts.

It sustains (controls) the launching of a new enterprise.

It's the nurturing process in the growth and development stage.

Before we talk about the credit side, I will try to make an argument for the great need of money and the resources to start and run you business. As I talk with business leaders and aspiring business owners, they all say they must have money.

Unfortunately, entrepreneurs typically start with the idea that if they had the money, they could start and operate their business. But do they want to do what is needed to get the money? Lets talk about that. Remember, it's business.

Entrepreneurs can acquire financing under very different conditions, from very different institutions, for very different periods of time. I talk about readiness, the position that you have placed yourself in to be considered for financing. It's not a given just because you have an idea.

The first step in financing a business is to determine how much money you will need to launch the business and keep it going until it can be expected to operate profitably. Let me stop for a minute and share or kill a myth. I am sure you have heard that a business should show a loss for the first three years when reporting to the IRS.

If that is to be true, then at what stage will a business become profitable? To whom would you want to show your financial statements while in search of funding? Keep it business without short cuts.

One of the key decisions that entrepreneurs who are starting a new business must make is where and how to acquire funds. There are a couple of rules of thumb to follow. Price is important, but it's not the only consideration. As in purchasing other goods and services, compare cost in acquiring financing, and look for the low cost source. But the cheapest may not be the best. It may have the wrong terms, onerous conditions, or inappropriate repayment schedules.

All these consideration normally don't matter at the hint that money is about to pass hands. But it should, and any true entrepreneur would really consider the cost. I have gotten a number of people upset with me because I will not agree with them on financial decisions.

The questions to ask are simple: Does the need out-weigh the cost? Can the perception of the need be over-rated? Is there another way to deal with this need? Paying three times the actual cost is okay to some. They are simply the ones who are not truly ready.

Now, if it is not going to cost you much, you also need to have some questions to ask. If you have no questions, then be very sure that you fully understand the terms and conditions. It can break you down just as much as the cost.

I really feel that those of you who listen to my radio show or have read any of my other books must know and see a connection. It is very similar to how you access your personal finances. Many of the decision are made the same way.

Generally, you should borrow funds for periods that are close to the useful life of the purpose of the funds. You do not need a degree in finance to understand that.

When you buy a house, you do not finance it with a bankcard. You look for a 30-year mortgage. But I must be honest and tell you that there may be someone out there trying to suggest or teach that you can.

Conversely, you do not get a 30-year financing to pay for new clothes. Automobile loans have terms on the order of four years because they are structured to parallel with the life of the car.

The same principles should apply in business. But the range of choices is much wider. Therefore, you must police yourself in making a decision regarding the type of terms you will agree to.

To help you with that, I have listed a number of funding resources that can possibly help determine what is best for your business. The next chapter and next page, talks about the funding choices and the factors.

Chapter 4

Funding Sources

Almost all business owners have several types of funding choices, which are based on various factors about their business. Some of the programs are available through banks and private lending, regardless of the nature of your business.

Here are some of the sources:

- **SBA** - Loans to small businesses from private-sector lenders (banks, etc.), which are guaranteed by the SBA.
  The SBA has no funds for direct lending or loans to small businesses with long-term, fixed-rate financing for major fixed assets, such as land and buildings.
- **Secured** - Working Capital - Seeking to convert company or personal assets into working capital. Giving a security in an asset(s) in exchange for cash.
- **Unsecured - Working Capital** - Loans for working capital that are unsecured and only based on the credit worthiness of the applicant.
- **Commercial Real Estate** - Commercial real estate loan with fixed or variable terms.
- **Accounts Receivable Factoring** - Accounts receivable serve as collateral for short-term working capital loans that you can obtain fast and cost effectively.
- **Franchise Start-ups** - Specialized financing reserved for the franchisees of recognized, typically nationally known, franchises.
- **Business Acquisitions** - Loan to acquire an existing business
- **Lines of Credit** - A pre-arranged amount of credit based upon existing inventory, A/R and PO's or up to $200,000 in business credit based upon credit worthiness with no collateral.
- **Professional Loans for Doctors, Dentists, Lawyers, CPAs, etc**.

- **Equipment Financing** - Loans to purchase equipment, with the equipment to be used as the collateral on the loan.
- **Equipment Sale-Lease Back** - If you have existing equipment, sell it and then lease back the equipment. Essentially you get cash for your equipment and then you lease it back from the lender.

- **Equipment Leasing** - An easier way to find financing for your equipment needs and obtain tax benefits at the same time.

- **Construction Financing** - Loans for home or commercial construction.
- **Residential Equity Lines** - Lines of credit secured by the equity in your residence.
- **Residential Mortgage Lending** - Loans for residential homes at the current interest rates in the market place.
- **Hard Money Equity Loans** - Loans available, those are typically hard to obtain from a local bank lender.
- **Multi-Family Real Estate Loans** - Loans for real estate investors. As you can see from the loans above there are many variables that can make lending possible. These types of loans are considered collateral type loans for the most part. Yet there may be other variables that may be required. Be careful.

Using Banks Finance

For most entrepreneurs, banks are the crucial source of financing. These institutions are called " commercial banks," after all, because their primary business has always been financing commerce.

Banks provide a vast array of short and medium term financing. You can arrange individual loans with a wide variety of interest rates and repayment schedules.

For many businesses, however, it's more efficient to arrange a revolving line of credit. Essentially, the bank reviews you and your business and determines a maximum amount it will lend you. Then you can borrow as much of that sum as you need when you need it; as you repay it, you can borrow more. It's not like your Visa or MasterCard, where you have a predetermined credit limit.

More established business owners and entrepreneurs obtain credit on the basis of their own reputation and the track record of their business. Essentially, the bank has enough confidence in the entrepreneurs or business owner and the business to provide money in return for signing an IOU.

Entrepreneurs who are unknown are typically asked to provide collateral for their loans. Just as a specific house secures a home mortgage and a car secures an automobile loan, secured business borrowing is tied to specific assets-real estate of vehicles or equipment. If you do not repay, the bank can foreclose on the collateral.

Banks will request all kinds of financial data in connection with a business loan, but the loan decision is in fact, highly judgmental. That can be frustrating, but it also means that if one bank turns down your loan application, another bank may approve it. In seeking bank financing, it pays to understand the characteristics and attributes of different banks, and seek funds from the right bank.

Banks not only have different degrees of risk tolerance but rather different areas of specialization. Some banks have more experience with smaller businesses than others. Some have more experience with specific industries. And some have more experience with specific types of financing.

The more experience they have, often the more comfortable they are in certain areas. Thus, it pays to find banks that are familiar with situations like yours because they're more apt to provide financing for it.

By the same token, if you have done business of any kind with a particular bank, you should approach that bank in seeking financing for your business venture. This is where that banking relationship that you read or hear me talking about really makes a difference.

The relationship you have with the bank may be in a business that is completely different from your new business. Nonetheless, because the bank is acquainted with you, this will play a beneficial role in the bank's assessment of your quest for financing.

In short, in seeking credit from a bank, remember there are lots of banks. Your best bet is to go to the ones that already know something about your proposal, either because they know you, they know the business, or they know the industry or geographic area in which your prospectus business will operate.

Also, in addition to traditional bank financing, new businesses should examine a whole array of other sources of financing for businesses, including various kinds of commercial finance companies as well as leasing companies, factors, and others. These may b independent institutions, although many have become subsidiaries of commercial banks.

Typical bank loans are based on an analysis of the financial history of a business, but new businesses don't have any history. Most non-bank financing is asset-based, which means the credit is made available because particular assets secure it. This kind of financing comes in various forms.

Need for personal credit history - Most business loans require a review of the personal credit history of the owners or applicants of the business loan and a personal guarantee. It is possible to avoid this however; in most cases this is required. One way to avoid the personal credit checks and guarantees is to use trade credit. I will tell you more about trade credit a little later.

Business Only Loans - Loans are available to obtain in the business name only without the use of personal credit, as long as the business can justify the loan amount and ability to pay it back. This must be a part of your original plan. If not, it could very well be apart of what you can do if your business has been operating for some time.

Financing Secured By Receivables
Commercial financial companies may provide loans by specifying that as customers make payments, these receivables go directly to the finance company to pay down the loan. Because they have a first call on these payments, they are comfortable lending to new companies and entrepreneurs.

In this financing, the lender is taking a risk not on you but rather on your customers; it is their timely payments for your goods or services that will repay your obligation.

Equipment Leasing

Most entrepreneurs and small business owners understand the value of renting or leasing equipment for operating reasons. If you need more trucks on Friday than you do on the rest of the week, don't buy extra trucks, just rent them on Friday.

But leasing is also a financing tool. Rather than buying equipment, you can order it from a leasing company, which will purchase it and deliver it to you. The equipment company owns the equipment and takes the risk that the stream of lease payments, together with the residual value, is high enough to pay for the equipment.

In addition, the leasing company gets the tax benefits of owning the equipment. In their early stages, many businesses don't generate any profits and therefore can't use such tax benefits as depreciation anyway. Thus, leasing can be an effective way to acquire equipment at an attractive cost while conserving cash.

Moreover, leasing protects a business against the risk of equipment becoming obsolete. At, the end of the lease term, the leasing company, rather than the leasor, has to bear the risk that the equipment will be outdated and difficult to resell.

With any of the resources that you feel can help you, do your research. This becomes difficult only when you have not properly prepared you and your business for this stage. I know that I keep saying "It's Business, Not Personal." Yet I still refer back to you and the readiness that you must have.

Original Quote

Someone said good things come to those who wait. I know that they are the very things that are left behind by those who have hustled. Now, right this moment you decided should you wait on it or should you hustle for it.

The mindset that you begin with establishes where you will end up. So, which is it? Wait or Hustle. "It's Business Not Personal"

Robert Wilson

Chapter 5

Prepare You and Your Business

Here I go again....I know that I keeping saying, "It's Business, Not Personal," and it *really* is. The fact of the matter is simple; in business there is a demand for a character check. That may involve your personal information. That does not mean that it will require a personal guarantee on a loan.

Do not be fooled though, your personal information will always be the foundation of anything you do financially. Therefore, develop it, as you should do any way. If you can be successful with your personal credit, then when it comes to your business credit you will say, "Bring it on baby!" I will show you some possible ways to develop business credit outside of the window of good.

Remember, that as you go, so goes your business. Any form of compromise can completely jeopardize your ability to live and build your dream. I believe that this is where the great divide is established. This is where a successful business begins to leave behind the failing business by leaps and bounds. Items lenders will look for to obtain a loan using personal information are:

- Personal Credit Score and Profile
- Age of Credit History
- Available Revolving Credit
- Applicants Ability to Pay Back the Loan
- Personal Financial Statements
- Personal Tax Returns
- Any of the Items Listed with the Business Requirements
- Down Payment
- Have a favorable business credit score and personal score
- Business trade references
- Business bank account
- Do the research on what type of loan or lease you need

Develop a Plan

- Determine what business structure to use before applying for the loan or lease
- Determine why you need the money
- Determine how much you need
- Determine how you will pay it back

Put Together a Written Plan

Develop in writing an executive summary of the loan or lease you're looking for. Prepare a business plan and a marketing plan. Have two years financial statements and tax returns for the business and individually. If possible, almost any lender will want to see these three things before looking at an application.

Benefits of Leasing - Don't just focus on a business loan. In many instances a business lease may be more advantageous. Some of the benefits:

- No down payment
- Leasing offers the use of an asset, without the large down payment associated with ownership.
- The monthly lease payments under an operating lease are typically tax deductible.
- When leasing, you have the opportunity to preserve bank lines and working capital.
- Leasing enables you to replace outdated equipment with up to 100% financing including installation costs.
- It improves your cash flow, enabling you to gain more production and giving you a hedge against obsolescence.
- When you lease, you establish new lines of credit while generating a return on available cash and improving balance sheet ratios.
- Leasing also streamlines bookkeeping procedures,
- It expands your budget capabilities while avoiding costly financing delays.
- Leasing enables you to finance new machinery and equipment, or to turn presently owned equipment into cash.
- Replace technologically outdated machinery and equipment while preserving your cash and credit lines.

Packaging the Request

Before submitting any loan or lease request to a lender, you must have a package developed. The package must include what the lender is looking for. Each lender is different, which is why we recommend using our services. We know what each lender requires for their package and which lender meets your qualifications.

Lenders want the loan or lease request presented in a specific manner. Use a professional loan mentor who has several lenders to shop your request. The mentor will provide the lender what they want to see and that will increase your chances of approval. The mentor will also save you time and money.

Finding the Best Business Loan or Lease
It can be extremely difficult to find someone willing to give your business a loan or lease, without the proper credit profile. Before looking for financing, make sure you are prepared to present the offer to a lender.

Alternatives Available if You Don't Qualify

If you do not have the ability to obtain a business loan or find that lenders keep turning you down, there are alternatives. The first is to determine exactly what you will need the money for. By determining the use of funds you can decide if trade credit will help.

Trade credit is financing provided by other businesses to yours. Trade credit is the single largest business-to-business financing in the world. It is also one that is the last looked at and one of the easiest to obtain.

Trade Credit - Trade credit is referred to as Business Credit. Businesses will lend money to you to purchase their products if you qualify. Most businesses will look at your business credit profile and score to determine if you qualify. In most instances, when a loan is needed, it is to purchase products or services for the business.

It is at this point that a business could obtain the product or servic on credit if their business had a proper Business Credit Profile and Score.

Businesses turn to various credit bureaus to find the profile and score. Before you apply for business credit you should be certain you have a credit profile and score set up. This will increase your chances for approval.

Build Your Business Credit - Every business has the ability to build their business credit profile and score with the various business credit reporting agencies. These agencies each have a differer way of obtaining the information for the profile and formula to determine a business credit score.

It is important to work with professional coaches to walk you through the steps of building your business credit. The most impo tant reason is to avoid a High-Risk status with the credit bureaus.

All business credit bureaus will do checks on your business that the business must pass in order to receive a profile. Many business owners have no idea the checks are being performed until it is too late.

If the credit bureau doesn't find what they are looking for or finds something out of the ordinary, your business will be unable t obtain the credit it deserves. There is a maze of steps that Business Credit Services can walk you through to obtain the credit profile and score.

CHAPTER 6

Becoming A Vendor

How To Do Business With the County

In this chapter I am going to give you some general information about another source of funding. This type can create many opportunities to grow your business. If I had to point to a source, this would be it.

This is another one of the great divides in the business world. Many mom and pop businesses never really get off the ground because they never chose to look at this area as a resource. Therefore they remain a mom and pop operation.

Let me also challenge you to consider and enlarge your scope in this area. Learn the information and in the process of you getting yourself in a readiness position look at the corporate market as well.

Take a look at WalMart and consider the process and how most of the requirements are very similar. What it would take to get your product or service tied to that company?

There are a number of corporation that you could possibly take a hard look. Having set-up your business credit with the appropriate business credit reporting and the information that you are about to learn could have you in the right position.

I know that many of you have heard about such programs and will not want to consider them; that is all right. The poor will forever be with us, maybe because of some the decision that they will and have made.

Remember that the federal government and your state and local governments all have a stake in the nurturing of new and small businesses. Did nurturing come back to your mind a minute ago?

When we talk about the "Mother's Milk," that was one of the things I asked you to focus on. If you forgot or if you have been skipping around go back for a moment to page 11 and 12 and read it again.

The nurturing of new and small businesses by governmental agencies has proven to be the best way to create new jobs. New businesses also pay taxes, help revitalize neighborhoods, and bring even more businesses to a locality.

Because of the critical role that new businesses play in maintaining and expanding an economy, governments have a number of programs to encourage and assist new businesses.

You should familiarize yourself with these programs and use them effectively.

The following steps are necessary to do business with County Government:

1. Secure a Vendor Application form from the County Department of Purchasing. They will mail you a Vendor Application upon request. You may also obtain an electronic Vendor Application form from the County website.

2. Follow the instructions on the application form. Complete all requested information and return the application to the Department of Purchasing.

3. Your application will be processed. You will be assigned a vendor code and your company (or your name) will be placed on the County's unified bidder's list for the goods or service(s) you provide.

4. Counties require that a vendor be licensed to do business with the County.

5. Based on the information you provide and items you select in your completed Vendor Application, the Department of Purchasing can inform you, through the County's Invitation to Bid/Request for Proposal/Request for Quotation notices, of prospective projects and contracting opportunities.

6. County's bid opportunities and procurement results can be viewed from the County's website. In addition, the County's formal Bid/Proposal solicitations (i.e. purchases of $50,000 and higher) are advertised in local publications for at least two (2) consecutive weeks. Public viewing of bid opportunities and procurement results is also available by visiting the Department of Purchasing.

The following provides an understanding of the County's procurement process:

All requisitions for goods and services from County departments are received in and processed by the Department of Purchasing, except for the County Public School System and the County Housing Authority.

For procurements that have a monetary value of $ .01 to $2,499.99, no bids or quotes are required as established by State laws and County ordinance. Buyers who are assigned to the Department of Purchasing selects vendors randomly from the unified bidder's list or by using suggested vendors from the User Department.

For procurements that have a monetary value of $2,500 to $49,999.99, a minimum of five (5) quotes must be solicited by the Department of Purchasing from five (5) vendors.

For procurements that have a monetary value of $50,000 and higher, a formal sealed bid (Invitation To Bid) or proposal (Request For Proposal) solicitation is required and a legal notice must be published in a newspaper of general circulation.

- The Bid/Proposal document is sent to Purchasing by the User Department
- The Project is advertised
- A pre-bid/proposal conference may be held
- Bids are publicly opened and read; for RFP's only the names of submitting firms are read
- The User Department selects and recommends the lowest responsible and responsive bidder to the County Manager and the Board of Commissioners

- A County Vendor Selection Committee reviews and recommends the selection of a vendor(s) in response to a Request For Proposal (RFP) solicitation to the County Manager and the Board of Commissioners

All vendor bids/proposals are due in to the Department of Purchasing on the date and time specified in the solicitation. Late bids/proposals are not accepted.

It is the mission of Purchasing & Contracting to provide fair and equal treatment to all persons, both County departments and vendors, involved in the procurement process.

All contracts for the purchase or lease of goods, services, insurance or construction are awarded through competitive bidding or negotiations, or through other processes established by Federal statutes, State law, and City and County Codes.

Overview of the Purchasing Process

Purchasing & Contracting utilizes a competitive bidding process, with awards made to the lowest responsible, responsive bidder, meeting the specifications. This process is called Invitation to Bid (ITB).

Questions regarding Invitations to Bid and Request for Proposal must be <u>submitted in writing, via email, fax, or mail</u> to the Purchasing & Contracting Department in time to allow a written response to all bidders in the form of addenda. This is to ensure that all Bidders receive the same information. Oral explanations or instructions will not be binding.

Submitting Your Bids

Informal bids may be submitted by telephone, mail, or in person to the Purchasing & Contracting Department, as requested.

Formal sealed bids for items greater than a particular dollar amount is to be submitted to the Purchasing & Contracting Department <u>not later than</u> the date and time set for opening. Bids received after deadline is not considered.

It is incumbent upon the bidder to ensure that bids are filled out correctly, completely and signed. Double-check prices; (most bids should be in unit prices). Ensure that all requirements are submitted with your bid, such as bonds, samples (at no cost to the County), literature, references, time payment discounts considered for 20 days or more, etc.

Prices submitted for Indefinite Quantity Contracts are to be firm prices for one year. If a firm price cannot be given, an escalation clause with a not-to-exceed percent increase must be given. However, the County may or may not accept escalation clauses depending on other bids received.

Remember that Indefinite Quantity Contracts are based on estimated quantities with orders placed by the County on an as-needed basis through the contract period. Be sure that delivery/completion date can be met. Any item (such as samples) submitted with the bid should be clearly marked as to item, invitation number, vendor, etc. (NOTE: samples may not be returned.)

Bid openings are public. You and/or representative of your firm are welcome to attend whether your firms engaged in bidding or not. Information regarding sealed bid prices; will be given over telephone or written as requested after they have been opened, abstracted and checked.

It is the goal of all employees in the Purchasing & Contracting Department to obtain the very best value for every tax dollar spent for the County and to ensure that your visit to this department is productive and pleasant.

Awarding of Contracts.

Contracts are awarded based on a combination of factors, which are most advantageous to that County. Those Counties reserves the right to make no awards, one award of all items or multiple awards of items. The method utilized to solicit bids and proposals is determined by the estimated dollar value of the individual purchase or the type of commodity or service needed.

Doing business with the state

Most State's conducts business with many private-sector companies, known as vendors. Vendors compete by bidding against each other for state contracts. Contract areas range from which Software Company will be used to develop an application to which construction company or contractor will build new state buildings or roadways.

To become a vendor to the state, businesses must register with the state before they are allowed to enter bids for certain state accounts. To register, prospective vendors need to send their name, company name and e-mail address to the state.

There are several different types of bids, including information technology, statewide contracts, consulting, construction, commodities, services and miscellaneous bids.

Doing Business with City Government

The following steps are necessary to do business with City.

- Secure a Bidder's Application Package from the Department of Procurement ("DOP"). Follow the instructions in the package, complete all the requested information, and return the application.
- Your application will then be processed. You will be issued a vendor number and your name will be placed on the City's bidder's list for the service(s) that you provide.
- Once you are awarded a contract, the City requires a vendor to be licensed to do business in that state. A City license may be obtained also.
- The Office of Contract Compliance ("OCC") is another office that plays an important role in the bid process. The Contract Employment Report Form ("CER") found in the Bidder's OCC. Additionally reviews Application Package; certification for minority and female business enterprise status is handled through OCC.
- Based on the information you provide and the items you select in the application, DOP will inform you, by its Invitation to Bid notices, of projects out-for-bid or proposals. Additionally, all projects by DOP are advertised in local publications for two (2) consecutive weeks.

Understanding the competitive sealed bid/proposal process

This is where the rubber met the road. By not understanding this process can cost you on both end of the business. Lost time and energy for not meeting requirements. Lost revenue that could have been generated with a contract.

Read and understand the process below. This is a typical outline of with city, county, state and federal Governments. Always be sure to check out their process and understand it.

- The bid document is sent to DOP by the user agency.
- The project is advertised.
- The pre-bid/proposal conference is held, when applicable.
- The vendor/contractor's bid submittals are due to DOP in accordance with the bid documents.
- The bids are publicly opened and read by DOP staff.
- For proposals, the names of the proponents are read publicly.
- The user agency reviews the bid/proposal submittals.
- A recommendation is submitted, by the user agency and OCC, to DOP for contract award.
- The CPO, in consultation with the user agency, then recommends the award of a contract.
- DOP prepares appropriate legislation for award, when applicable.
- DOP prepares the appropriate contractual agreement/purchase order.
- The contract agreement is forwarded to the contractor and a purchase order is issued.
- The vendor/contractor signs the contract and provides the appropriate bonding and insurance information.
- Once signed by the contractor, the contract is routed internally for the appropriate signatures.
- The contract is officially executed after the Municipal Clerk seals it.
- Copies of the contract are distributed to the appropriate parties.
- Finally, a Notice to Proceed ("NTP") is issued to the contractor to begin the work.

Original Quote

This is how my mother always has done.

I do not need anybody.

I have to do this myself.

I know, I had my own business before.

Whenever you begin to think that you do not need guidance or direction from others, consider the statements above. Then find a way to reverse the way you think and do the opposite. This is your chance to take what hinders you and set it aside.

Robert Wilson

Chapter 7

Business Credit Card

This is an area that I receive thousand of question about. Often times I wonder if I should even comment or answer. So, first I will give my comments about the Business Credit Cards and what I feel may be important.

I will point out that many of you may already have business credit cards and may have different experiences and opinions. That is quite all right. What is most important is the fact that you learn more about them.

It's now again personal. Whenever you think of owning a credit card of any type, the first thing you must realize is the condition and principles that credit card operate under. They are a profit driven company. That really sounds strange to say that it is a profit driven company.

Are not all businesses a profit driven company of some type? Well, yes and no. Yes, because many of them simply operate with standards that allow them to make decisions based on risk. The manner that they associate you to their product indicates to them the potential profit that they will make.

Based on their standards, they will extend credit accordingly. There may be a tier system in place and based on the risk factors, there could be four levels. These four levels establish the forecasted profits for the company. Because of their ownership and proprietary rights, I will say this in my own words.

Level One - *Exceptional* - You will qualify for their highest credit line and their lowest rate. You may even receive rebates and extra air miles.

Level Two- *Low Risk* - A step down may give you basically the same as level one. The rebates and perks may not be available to you. The rates here may also have some footnotes that allow the interest rates to change. This level is more common among new businesses that are developing business credit.

Level Three- *Medium Risk* - is where you find the game somewhat changes. The line of credit is reduced; the terms and condition have gone into a protective mode. Rebates and air miles seem to be something to hope for one day. This level in normally perk free and has higher interest rates.

Level Four- *High Risk* - simple lower credit lines and higher interest rates. I could stop here, but I will continue. Absolutely no perks or rebates of any kind. The terms and conditions dare you to miss a payment. Rates will hit the ceiling as soon as you slip. This is their most profitable product.

You see this is Business 101. Securing your profit bottom line. There is always a more profitable product in every business. As an entrepreneur, you should and must understand this. So, the answer is **Yes** to businesses being a profit driven company.

However, I also said **No**. There are so many business owner and entrepreneur that just want to keep the business running. If they could pay the rent this month they will try to improve the next month. If they could just get this bill paid, things will be all right for a while.

It seems to always be something that is needed to get pass a situation. There is always an excuse that justifies failure. These types of businesses and entrepreneurs run rampant in communities. They are also the ones that are quick to blame others for their inability to see a profit. I'll shut up here, but I think you get the picture.

On the next page, I put together some questions and answers for those of you who did not get what you have just read. I'll also include some of the benefits that come along with level one.

Even if your personal credit is required, consider how to now best use it. The game should be the same on both sides. If they are consistence in their efforts to make a profit, then you likewise should go into this thing with the same idea.

This really should not be new information. It really just should be about business. After all if you are reading this book, you are trying to take your business to another level, right? **It is business.**

Business Card – Questions and Answers

1. How should I use this card?

Use it exclusively for your business - the same way you use a credit card for personal use. To better control expenses and simplify bookkeeping, you and your key employees should each have a Business Card.

2. What is the credit limit?

You may be approved for up to $50,000. You can order separate cards for you and your employees. You determine the credit limit for each card.

3. What is the interest rate?

The interest rate for purchases will be between Prime + 4% and Prime +14%, depending on your personal and business credit evaluation. Prime refers to the Prime Rate. The interest rate for cash advances is Prime + 12% with a 19.8% minimum. If you default under the Customer Agreement, the interest rate applied to all balances may be increased to a rate up to Prime + 14%, subject to a minimum of 21.99%.

4. What's your minimum monthly payment?

It is equal to the total of interest and fees ($10 minimum) plus any over limit/past due amount. See Cardholder Agreement for details.

5. Can I use this line for overdraft protection?

Yes, if you link it up to a business checking account. (One checking account per credit card, please.)

6. Do I need an account to get a Business Card?

No. With the Business Card, you may repay by writing a check or making an automatic transfer from any business checking account you have at virtually any bank.

7. Is there a fee?

There is no annual fee for the most Visa Business Card. An Inactive Account Fee of $25 will be assessed to each card used fewer than 1? times during the immediately preceding anniversary year. The annual fee for the program is $50 per business.

8. What are your chances of being approved?

Each case is different. Your chances are helped if you've been in business for at least three years, or just two years if you're a customer. It also helps if your business is profitable and if you have a good personal and business credit history

Secured Business Cards

1. What is the Business Secured Card Account and how does it work?
The Business Secured Card account is a revolving line of credit secured by a cash deposit into a security deposit account. It works like any other business credit card account.

2. Why is a Business Security Deposit Account required?
The security deposit account will act as collateral for your Business Secured Card account.

3. Will I qualify for Card benefits with this Business Account?
With the Business Secured Card account, you'll get valuable Card benefits such as
- Insurance Coverage
- Purchase Assurance / Extended Warranty
- Travel Assistance Services

(Be sure to read the terms and conditions associated with each.)

4. What is the credit limit?
Your credit limit is equal to the value of the funds you deposit in your security deposit account. The minimum is $1,000 and the maximum is $100,000. Also, once your account is set up, you can make additional deposits and your credit limit will increase by that amount.

5. What is the interest rate on the Business Secured Card Account?
The interest rate will be Prime + 9.9% for purchases. If you make your payments within the grace period, you can minimize or avoid any interest payments! If you default under the Customer Agreement, the interest rate applied to all balances may be increased to a rate up to Prime + 14%, subject to a minimum of 21.99%.

6. Will I earn interest on the Security Deposit Account?
The interest rate for the security deposit is 2.5% during the first year and 0.5% thereafter (rates subject to change).

7. What will be the minimum monthly payment?
It is equal to the total of interest and fees ($10 minimum) plus any amount past due.

8. Can I use the Business Secured Card Account For Overdraft Protection?
Yes, if you link it up to a business checking account.

9. Can I get a Business Secured Card Account even if I don't already have an account with our company?
Yes, you can get a Business Secured Card account without having an account. And it's a great way to begin your relationship with their company.

10. What is the annual fee?
The annual fee is just $25 per card. The annual fee for the program is $50 per business.

11. What if your existing or new business had problems getting credit in the past?
There are only a few reasons for not approving an application, such as declaring bankruptcy within the past 12 months from the application date. Most people who apply for a Business Secured Card account are able to open the account.

12. Can I get cash advances on the Business Secured Card?
Cash may be advanced from the Business Secured Card account by presenting the Business Card at a financial institution that accepts credit cards when your outstanding balance (including cash advances) does not exceed 50% of the credit limit. The Annual Percentage Rate for cash advances is 's Prime Rate + 12%, subject to a minimum of 19.8%.

13. Can I Cancel?
You can cancel your account at any time. Your security deposit account will be refunded when all outstanding charges have been paid.

Corporate Card

1. What is the Corporate Card?
It is an innovative management tool for your business. With only one card, you'll now be able to manage and track your general purchasing, travel and entertainment costs, and vehicle expenditures. The Corporate Card's easy to use reporting options allow you to track and understand your company's expenses more completely.

2. How can I most effectively use the Corporate Card?
Many of them can help you match cards with job functions. With the Corporate Card, each card can be set to allow purchases that are unique to an employee's job function. For example, you might set a salesperson's card to allow only purchases for travel, hotels, and meals. For route drivers, the card would allow purchases for fuel and vehicle maintenance.

3. What will be your credit line?
The Corporate Card offers a credit line from $20,000 to $250,000 per account. Individual credit lines can range from $250 to $25,000 per card.

4. Can I use this line for overdraft protection?
No.

5. What will be your interest rate?
The interest rate associated with the Corporate Card is Prime plus a range from 0% to 9.8% depending on your personal and business credit history.

6. What will be your minimum monthly payment?
Your minimum monthly payment is 2% of the current balance, or $10 minimum, plus any past-due amount.

7. Do I need to be a customer to qualify for the Corporate Card?
No. But your chance for credit approval increases if you have another account.

8. Is there an annual fee for the Corporate Card?
Yes. The number of cards determines fees. The annual fee is only $10 per card for 1 to 50 cards. There is no annual fee if you have more than 50 cards.

9. What are your chances of being approved?
A review of your application is necessary for approval. In each situation, the application must meet the Bank's underwriting criteria. They look for businesses with at least a three-year track record and good personal and business credit history. Your business must be profitable.

How Some Make Our Lending Decisions

Building your credit is important to growing your business. They feel that the more you know, the better your chances will be in securing business credit. The following are important questions you should consider before you apply for credit.

1. Are you the principal decision-maker for your business?
If you are, they will ask you to complete and submit the loan application. If there are multiple owners of your business, at least two of them will need to submit their information with the application.

2. Have you been in business at least three years?

Your financial performance over time is usually a pretty good measure of where you've been and where you're going. To get conventional bank financing, it helps to have been in business for at least three years.

3. Have you filed for bankruptcy within the past 10 years?

If either you or your business has declared bankruptcy within the last 10 years, chances are they will not lend to you - unless you have repaid all of your creditors. The best way for you to re-establish a good credit record is to repay your creditors as soon as possible.

4. Have you consistently paid your bills - both business and personal - on time?

Uses a business credit-reporting agency to see how you have paid your trade suppliers and other business obligations. Many use a consumer credit-reporting agency to see how you have handled your personal debt.

While an occasional late or missed payment is understandable, if you consistently pay late, you may not qualify for business credit. Sometimes you just need to set up an accounting system to ensure that you pay all your bills on schedule.

If you find that you are consistently running short of cash, then you should take steps to trim expenses, increase sales revenues or raise equity for your business.

5. Is there a tax lien, suit or judgment against you or your business?

In the case of a tax lien or a legal judgment against you or your firm, the beneficiary of any settlement stands first in line for payment. The best thing to do before you apply for business credit is to pay and release all liens and judgments, and settle all suits.

6. Do you have five or more sources of credit?

Credit cards, lines of credit, and loans are a key part of every individual's credit record. A strong credit history proves you have the willingness and discipline to repay debts.

Lack of a credit record makes it much more difficult to borrow money. If you do not have credit today, secure credit soon and use it wisely. Good places to start include trade credit, credit cards, auto loans, home equity and lines of credit.

7. Has your business been profitable for the last two years?

Tax returns are a quick way to determine if you've shown a profit in the last few years. If your business is not profitable, it may be difficult for you to make the payments on your credit line or loan. I talked about this, if your business is not profitable, examine your expenses for opportunities to cut back and look at your sales for opportunities to increase revenues. Maybe you can sell more to a current customer, or you might need more customers.

8. Does your business generate at least $1.50 in cash flow for every $1 you pay out to cover expenses?

Looks at the cash your business generates as the primary repayment source for the money you borrowed. They compute the cash in your business by adding non-cash expenses (such as depreciation and amortization) to net profits.

If your business doesn't generate $1.50 in cash for every $1 in debt payments, then you will need to look for ways to decrease expenses or increase sales to boost the cash in your business.

9. What are the five factors they use to assist us in making lending decisions?

Character. What kind of borrower will you be for the bank? The best clue to your character is your personal credit history. They always check to see how well you have managed your personal debt in the past.

What if you do not have personal credit history? Personal references, business experience and work history can sometimes substitute, but a strong personal credit history proves that you have the willingness and the discipline to repay past debts - and future obligations.

Credit. Uses a credit-reporting agency to look at your payment history with trade suppliers and other business obligations. They also look to see that your payments to other financial institutions are current.

Cash Flow. What is a cash flow lender? That means they look at the cash flow of your business as the primary repayment source for the money they lend you.

How do they compute cash flow? A company's cash flow is its net profit, plus its non-cash expenses - depreciation and amortization. Our rule of thumb is that for every $1 in total loan payments, your business must generate $1.50 in cash flow.

Capacity. Wants to know how you would be able to repay your loan in case there was a sudden downturn in your business. Do you have the capacity to convert other assets to cash, either by selling them or borrowing against them?

Your ability to do this could include real estate holdings, certificates of deposit, stocks and other sources of savings that can be liquidated quickly.

Collateral. This applies to both secured and unsecured loans. With a secured loan, you pledge something that you own as collateral. It might be personal assets like certificates of deposits or stocks, or business assets like real estate, inventory, and equipment or accounts receivable.

Chapter 8

Doing It My Way, "A Vision"

Business Credit

I put this at the end for a very good reason. The reason, in my opinion, to do this could be your great reward. If you just jump to this chapter, then you get what you get. You surely deserve it.

You will need what has been established and stated in all of the other chapters at some point. It is the funding processes that take a business to the next level. If you skipped to this section, good luck.

Now, those of you that have read up to this point want to know how to get credit established with your business. Also, you would like to do it on your business alone. That is what I will try to help you get a clear picture of in this chapter.

However, I must start by stating a number of facts and also give you some important information as well. Learn the facts and allow the information to work its course of gestation and germination.

First, let me start with the facts.

Business Credit Agencies

There are several business credit reporting agencies in the United States that lenders and financial institutions rely on for information to grant credit. Many businesses can take years before they are listed with the business credit agencies; some may never be listed.

Many past and current clients are not listed with any credit-reporting agency. The one that comes to mind is a member of my church and has been in business for 16 years and not one bureau had his company listed.

Some of these credit-reporting agencies are FDInsight, D&B, Experian Business, BusinessCreditUSA and ClientChecker. I want to give you a clear, concise, and brief description of each.

FDInsight

Is relatively new to the business credit market. It is fast and growing in the area of business credit reporting. Originally made its mark as a personal credit-reporting agency for mortgage brokers. They are the second largest credit reporting company in the mortgage broker field.

The business or a third party provides information on businesses and then the staff of FDInsight verifies every piece of information. They arguably provide the most accurate business credit report in the industry. The company is listed on NASDAQ as FDCC.

Dunn & Bradstreet

Over 70 million businesses are registered with D&B. The credit profile created by D&B uses information provided by the business owners and vendors of the business. Grants a PAYDEX score to businesses based on payment experiences of the business.

Issues a DUNS rating based on the financial statements of the business. Has a High Risk status for companies that will destroy their ability to obtain credit if D&B finds information on a company they feel to be inconsistent with their model. Pound for pound the very best.

Experian Business

Over 14 million businesses are registered with Experian. The credit profile created by Experian, uses information provided by vendors only. Grants an Intelliscore based on payment experiences. One of the three largest personal credit bureaus that you should already be familiar with.

BusinessCreditUSA

A division of InfoUSA provides inexpensive business credit reports. Relies on information from the business owner to report vendor's relationships. Verifies all information presented to them before placing on the report. Please keep in mind that almost all of them verify information.

ClientChecker

The only credit-reporting agency dedicated to small businesses. The credit profile created by ClientChecker, uses information provided by vendors only. Grants a PayQuo Score based on payment experiences. Enables vendors to report on all aspects of working with business, for a more complete picture.

I am willing to bet that most of you have all already learned something regarding the credit-reporting agencies for business credit. If you notice, very little if any references to personal credit were a part of these descriptions.

Knowing who the credit-reporting agencies are allows you a great opportunity to research and discover how they operate as you start your journey. The more the merrier could also be one's prospective. I do not believe, however, that each of them can help all of you. There is and will be one suited just to your business needs. That is the one that you do primarily all of your business with. Do not just limit yourself.

If you see that most of your vendors are with a credit-reporting agency that you are not, then do not pack your bags and move. Instead, add that credit-reporting agency to your other relationships. Use the facts in this chapter as a guide.

Now, its time for the information part that you are waiting for. This may be the part, which many of you only wanted anyway. I say that because you want it fast and right now.

Business Credit Scores

The business credit scores are what the lenders and financial institutions look for to determine credit worthiness of a business. The score alone will not determine approval of a loan or lease.

Many factors will be reviewed to determine approval. As with a business credit profile, a score too can take several years to obtain. Many businesses never obtain a score, because they don't know it's available or they don't know how to get one.

Before I begin to tell you how you can get one, I want to share with you a little more about them. There are currently three companies that provide a business credit score. I was not able to get the facts on some of the companies; I share it with you any way what I have

The score and the rating is different. You can be rated and not have a score; but you cannot have a score and not be rated. All of this will be explained to you in this chapter.

Now let's go to the scores.

PAYDEX Score - D&B

The credit profile created by D&B uses information provided by the business owners and vendors of the business. Grants a PAYDEX score to businesses based on payment experiences of the business.

- Score ranges from **0 to 100**
- A score of **75+ is good**
- Based on **payment experiences** reported by vendors
- Need **minimum of 5 trade** references who report to D&B; can be as high as 8

Intelliscore

The credit profile created by Experian uses information provided by vendors only. Grants an Intelliscore based on payment experiences

- Score ranges from **0 to 100**
- A score of **75+ is good**
- Based on **payment experiences** reported by vendors
- Need a **minimum of 3 trade** references who report to Experian

PayQuo Score

The credit profile created by ClientChecker, uses information provided by vendors only. Grants a PayQuo Score based on payment experiences.

- Score ranges from **20 to 90**
- A score of **80+ is good**
- Based on **payment experiences** reported by vendors
- **Need 3 trade** references who report to ClientChecker

DUNS Rating

Issues a DUNS rating based on the financial statements of the business. This is something that you all need to have. The rubber meets the road here.

- Various rating schedules
- Based on **employee size** and **financial statements**
- Also takes into account **payment history**

Other Bureaus

Other bureaus do not have a specific scoring system to provide credit grantors. Some of the bureaus are working on a scoring model to implement in the future. The process does not change.

To go though this process your business must have the **readiness** that I have talked about. This is where it's not personal. I do know that the title of the book is catchy but this is for real.

Your business must pass through your research to determine all local, state and federal requirements are in place; must also go through research to determine all lender and credit bureau requirements are in place.

Your business must be registered with several business credit bureaus to start the development of your business credit profile, separate from you personally.

You should get a list of businesses that will offer your business credit without the use of business or personal credit checks or personal guarantees when you register.

Locate a list of businesses that will extend your business lines of credit and retail credit cards based on your business credit profile; that will extend credit to your business based on your business credit profile and score.

Have your management team review your financial statements. If you do not have a management team develop a team of business coaches. Keep your business out of the **No Credit status.**

That is really how business operates. Let's not be confused. I want to take you through this information with an idea of what can be done to answer the requirements. The setup of business credit that I will show may or may not work for you. Learn the way of my thinking anyway.

This could be the cutting edge for most of you. If you have gotten this far in the book and have not taken some steps toward correcting how you set-up your business, then please stop here. There is really no need for you to want to go further.

Now comes the part where business and personal credit are separated.

How you can do it.

I know how people enjoy a hook-up. Sometimes hook-ups are just a set-up for you to fail. No, I am not saying that the person giving you a hook-up is setting you up. What I am saying is simple, every hook-up could be a short cut and any short cut can cause you to miss something.

Hook-ups can be a wonderful thing when done right. Get out of the habit of receiving hook-ups and just do business. That means your every action is about results and profits. You will create a division among your current associate. This division should be anticipated and welcome well in advance.

There are going to come times when you must determine which road you will travel - the path of less resistance, or will you climb the mountain ahead. Get your mind set on what you must do. The willingness to have or be a business owner is not enough.

As we have talked about getting your business in a readiness position, you must also be there as well. I felt that I had to go there in order to try and make what I am about to say make sense. We will now use my theory to build your business credit separately from your personal credit.

I am a developer. I build and remodel homes. In the process of building homes I may use business relationships to get most of the work done. These relationships are with other business people that have a desire to grow their own business as well.

Yet we constantly work hard together and never really make the right moves. We remain in business for years and years and don't consider the measure of being in business. The path to less resistance is the direction that we want to go in. After all, I am making money, making real good money.

The relationships are also making money; it cannot get any better than this. This is so much the wrong decision and attitude to have as a business owner. By now you probably know and understand why.

The fact that you are okay with just having a business and making money is costing you a lot. Money that you do not see can and will hurt you.

There are so many small and home base businesses that will never see the light of day. The mentality is, as I just descried, is one of being in business just to really say that they are, in other words, making money to pay bills and to the keep the business operating.

To start a business to operate only just part time is like getting half dressed. Business is full-time, not a magical fit for you to pick and choose when and how to work.

Here I go again just writing what pop's in my head. The truth is that we really do not know. To set up standards to build a business could be just within your circle.

Your credit is key, but you have relationships with the resources that can help you, not just as a vendor, but also to keep you moving forward with your business.

Remember, I am a developer; my existing relationships must improve. If each of the business owners go and get the DNB (dunns) number that sets your business up as a vendor, then each of you will be prepared to do business.

With knowing how the business credit reporting set up works, you are required to do business with other venders. These vendors then report their relationship to the credit reporting agencies.

Now, as a developer I will have at least four vendors that can supply the equipment and tools that I will need to complete my project. These vendors are paid as agreed and they in turn report this information.

The relationship can be built with many vendors. Once you have registered your business, you will have access to the vendors that are already listed with the agency.

As you accumulate and honor the relationships and agreements (at least three to five of them), they will report your activity and then you will be provided a score with the agency.

As with your personal credit, as your report changes so will your score. Each one helping one - this is networking at its greatest. This is where it is demanded that you perform well. This is what some have seen for years and not understood.

This has nothing to do with race, creed, gender or sexual orientation. But, you can hear many different stories that say otherwise. If you look clearly at the system and the process, you would have to agree.

Business now becomes business among businesses. There is a reason why the entrepreneur must place his/her business in the correct position to do business with other listed businesses.

To truly separate your personal credit for your business credit will also determine how you form your company. If formed the wrong way, personal credit would be the only source of getting credit.

I said, "the wrong way", but is there really a wrong way to do business? Yes, I think that when a business owner goes about setting up their business, he/she must determine what type of legal structure that will be formed, not how to bet the IRS.

The way that the business is structured also determines which direction you must take to go after business credit. We have talked about a lot of business requirements and how they can best suit your business need.

You want business credit and you want it separate from your personal credit. Then I will seriously ask you to go back to page 5; reread that chapter. The way you learn to put your business in the readiness is how loans are made.

This is all about credit, right? So then, everything I have talked about in this book should give most of you a good start out of the gate. The way you make your decision in setting up the business properly brings forth the ability to get credit.

On the next few pages I would like to share some of the main ways to consider setting up the business. As you do so, please try to remember where the great divide is. It begins with not having the readiness that you are going to need.

The "Mother's Milk" should never mix with your personal money. There is a difference in your personal money and credit, separate from the business money and credit.

If you get nothing else from book, please try to remember to always separate your business from your credit. The fact that many has and still co-mingle their personal and business activities do not make it right.

You will encounter people that will always continue to do the things that they have always done in business. That still does not make it right. Challenge yourself daily to improve and move in a different direction.

Just because behavior is consistent does not mean that it is correct behavior. Something that I learn, when I took a twelve-week class the course was name Radical Love.

This course opened my eyes in so many ways. It showed me how I operated from consistent behavior that I learn as I was growing up. Regardless of how much I felt that I were the best husband and treating my wife in the best possible way, I still were not in the divide nature of God's Love towards my wife.

In short, I did the entire things that I witness growing up; many of them not even close to what God would have me do. I was what they called marinating in the lessons of my past.

In business, many are marinating in the things that they have learned. The type of things they refused to allow them to go to another level in their business. This is your time to do something different to make a difference.

Check out www.radicallove.org

Chapter 9

Types of Ownership Structures

Here, I want you to learn about the various types of legal structures available for your business: corporation, LLC, partnership and sole proprietorship.

Before you can decide on an ownership structure for your business, you must learn at least a little bit about how each structure works. Many times people would call my show and ask me what type of structure they should have; it is not just that simple. Here's a brief rundown of the most common forms of doing business:
- Sole proprietorship
- Partnership
- Limited partnership
- Limited liability company (LLC)
- Corporation (for-profit)
- Nonprofit corporation (not-for-profit)
- Cooperative.

Sole Proprietorships and Partnerships

For many new businesses, the best initial ownership structure is either a sole proprietorship or -- if more than one owner is involved -- a partnership.

A sole proprietorship is a one-person business that is not registered with the state as a limited liability company (LLC) or corporation. You don't have to do anything special or file any papers to set up a sole proprietorship -- you create one just by going into business for yourself.

Legally, a sole proprietorship is inseparable from its owner -- the business and the owner are one and the same. This means the owner of the business reports business income and losses on her personal tax return and is personally liable for any business-related obligations, such as debts or court judgments.

Similarly, a partnership is simply a business owned by two or more people that haven't filed papers to become a corporation or a limited liability company (LLC). No paperwork needs to be filed to form a partnership -- the arrangement begins as soon as you start a business with another person.

As in a sole proprietorship, the partnership's owners pay taxes on their shares of the business income on their personal tax returns and they are each personally liable for the entire amount of any business debts and claims.

Sole proprietorships and partnerships make sense in a business where personal liability isn't a big worry -- for example, a small service business in which you are unlikely to be sued and for which you won't be borrowing much money for inventory or other costs.

Limited Partnerships

Limited partnerships are costly and complicated to set up and run, and are not recommended for the average small business owner. One person or company usually creates limited partnerships, the "general partner," who will solicit investments from others -- who will be the limited partners.

The general partner controls the limited partnership's day-to-day operations and is personally liable for business debts (unless the general partner is a corporation or an LLC). Limited partners have minimal control over daily business decisions or operations and, in return, they are not personally liable for business debts or claims. Consult a limited partnership expert if you're interested in creating this type of business.

Corporations and LLCs

Forming and operating an LLC or a corporation is a bit more complicated and costly, but well worth the trouble for some small businesses. The main benefit of an LLC or a corporation is that these structures limit the owners' personal liability for business debts and court judgments against the business.

What sets the corporation apart from all other types of businesses is that a corporation is an independent legal and tax entity, separate from the people who own, control and manage it.

Because of this separate status, the owners of a corporation don't use their personal tax returns to pay tax on corporate profits -- the corporation itself pays these taxes. Owners pay personal income tax only on money they draw from the corporation in the form of salaries, bonuses and the like.

LLCs are similar to corporations because they also provide limited personal liability for business debts and claims. But when it comes to taxes, LLCs are more like partnerships: the owners of an LLC pay taxes on their shares of the business income on their personal tax returns.

Corporations and LLCs make sense for business owners who either 1) run a risk of being sued by customers or clients or run the risk of piling up a lot of business debts, or 2) have a good deal of personal assets they want to protect from business creditors.

Nonprofit Corporations

A nonprofit corporation is a corporation formed to carry out a charitable, educational, religious, literary or scientific purpose. A nonprofit can raise much-needed funds by receiving public and private grant money and donations from individuals and companies.

The federal and state governments do not generally tax nonprofit corporations on money they make that is related to their nonprofit purpose, because of the benefits they contribute to society.

Cooperatives

Some people dream of forming a business of true equals -- an organization owned and operated democratically by its members. These grassroots business organizers often refer to their businesses as a "group," "collective" or "co-op" -- but these are usually informal rather than legal labels.

For example, a consumer co-op could be formed to run a food stor a bookstore or any other retail business. Or a workers' co-op could be created to manufacture and sell arts and crafts.

Sole Proprietorships FAQ

If you operate as a sole proprietorship, <u>you and your business are legally inseparable</u>.

What is a sole proprietorship and how do I create one?

A sole proprietorship is a company with one owner that is not registered with the state as a limited liability company (LLC) or a corporation. In some states, a sole proprietorship is referred to as a DBA (doing business as), as in "José Smith, doing business as Smitl Heating and Air Conditioning."

Establishing a sole proprietorship is cheap and relatively uncompli cated. You don't have to file any papers to set it up -- you create a sole proprietorship just by going into business. In other words, if you'll be the only owner of the business you're starting, your business will automatically be a sole proprietorship, unless you incorporate it or organize it as an LLC.

Of course, you do have to get the same business licenses and permits as any other company that goes into the same business.

How are sole proprietorships taxed?

Unlike a corporation, a sole proprietorship is not considered separate from its owner for tax purposes. This means the sole proprietorship itself does not pay income tax; instead, the owner reports business income or losses on his or her individual income tax return.

Note that all business income is taxed to the owner in the year the business receives it, whether or not the owner removes the money from the business.

Are sole proprietors personally liable for business debts?

Legally, a sole proprietorship is inseparable from its owner -- the business and the owner are one and the same. As a result, the owner of a sole proprietorship is personally liable for the entire amount of any business-related obligations, such as debts or court judgments.

This means that if you form a sole proprietorship, creditors of the business can come after your personal assets -- your house or your car, for example -- to collect what the business owes them.

Sole Proprietorship Basics

If you're going into business on your own, the simplest legal structure is the sole proprietorship.

A sole proprietorship is a business that is owned by one person and that isn't registered with the state as a corporation or a limited liability company (LLC).

Sole proprietorships are so easy to set up and maintain that you may already own one without knowing it. For instance, if you are a freelance photographer or writer, a craftsperson who takes jobs on a contract basis, a salesperson who receives only commissions, or an independent contractor who isn't on an employer's regular payroll, you are automatically a sole proprietor.

However, even though a sole proprietorship is the simplest of business structures, you shouldn't fall asleep at the wheel. You may have to comply with local registration, business license, or permit laws to make your business legitimate. And you should look sharp when it comes to tending your business, because you are personally responsible for paying both income taxes and business debts.

Personal Liability for Business Debts

A sole proprietor can be held personally liable for any business-related obligation. This means that if your business doesn't pay a supplier, defaults on a debt, or loses a lawsuit, the creditor can legally come after your house or other possessions.

Example 1: Lester is the owner of a small manufacturing business. When business prospects look good, he orders $50,000 worth of supplies and uses them in creating merchandise. Unfortunately, there's a sudden drop in demand for his products, and Lester can't sell the items he has produced.

When the company that sold Lester the supplies demands payment he can't pay the bill. As sole proprietor, Lester is personally liable for this business obligation. This means that the creditor can sue him and go after not only Lester's business assets, but his personal property as well. This can include his house, his car, and his personal bank account.

Example 2: Shirley is the owner of a flower shop. One day Roger, one of Shirley's employees, is delivering flowers using a truck owned by the business. Roger strikes and seriously injures a pedestrian.

The injured pedestrian sues Roger, claiming that he drove carelessly and caused the accident. The lawsuit names Shirley as a codefendant. After a trial, the jury returns a large verdict against Shirley as owner of the business. Shirley is personally liable to the injured pedestrian. This means the pedestrian can go after all of Shirley's assets, business and personal.

By contrast, the law provides owners of corporations and limited liability companies (LLCs) with what's called "limited personal liability" for business obligations. This means that, unlike sole proprietors and general partners, owners of corporations and LLCs can normally keep their house, investments, and other personal property even if their business fails.

If you will be engaged in a risky business, you may want to consider forming a corporation or an LLC. You can learn more about limiting your personal liability for business obligations by reading Nolo's articles on corporations and LLCs.

Paying Taxes on Business Income

In the eyes of the law, a sole proprietorship is not legally separate from the person who owns it. The fact that a sole proprietorship and its owner are one and the same means that a sole proprietor simply reports all business income or losses on his or her individual income tax return -- IRS Form 1040 with Schedule C attached.

As a sole proprietor, you'll have to take responsibility for withholding and paying all income taxes -- something an employer would normally do for you.

This means paying a "self-employment" tax, which consists of contributions to Social Security and Medicare, and making payments of estimated taxes throughout the year.

Registering Your Sole Proprietorship

Unlike an LLC or a corporation, you generally don't have to file any special forms or pay any fees to start working as a sole proprietor. All you have to do is declare your business to be a sole proprietorship when you complete the general registration requirements that apply to all new businesses.

Most cities and many counties require businesses -- even tiny home-based sole proprietorships -- to register with them and pay at least a minimum tax. In return, your business will receive a business license or tax registration certificate.

You may also have to obtain an employer identification number from the IRS (if you have employees), a seller's license from your state, and a zoning permit from your local planning board.

If you do business under a name different from your own (such as "Custom Coding" instead of "J Smith Graphics"), you usually must register that name -- known as a fictitious, or assumed, business name -- with your county.

In practice, lots of businesses are small enough to get away with ignoring these requirements. But if you are caught, you may be subject to back taxes and other penalties.

Corporations FAQ

Answers to the most frequently asked questions about corporations: what they are, how they work, and whether or not you should incorporate your business.

What is a corporation?

A corporation is a type of business structure created and regulated by state law. What sets the corporation apart from all other types of businesses is that a corporation is an independent legal entity, separate from the people who own, control and manage it.

In other words, corporation and tax laws view the corporation as a legal "person," meaning that the corporation can enter into contracts, incur debts and pay taxes apart from its owners.

And there are other important characteristics that result from the corporation's separate existence: a corporation does not dissolve when its owners (shareholders) change or die, and the owners of a corporation are not personally responsible for the corporation's debts; this is called limited liability.

What is "limited liability" and why is it important?

If a business owner has "limited liability," it means that he or she is not personally responsible for business debts and obligations of the corporation. In other words, if the corporation is sued, only the assets of the business are at risk, not the owners' personal assets, such as their houses or cars.

Corporate owners must comply with certain corporate formalities and keep up with paperwork to maintain this limited liability privilege.

Limited liability has traditionally been associated with corporations, and is the main reason that most people consider incorporating. However, other business structures, such as limited liability companies (LLCs), now offer this limited personal liability to business owners. Sole proprietorships and general partnerships do not.

How are corporations different from partnerships, sole proprietorships and LLCs?

Unlike corporations, partnerships and sole proprietorships do not provide limited personal liability for business debts. This means that creditors of those businesses can go after the owners' personal assets to collect what's due.

However, organizing and operating a partnership or sole proprietorship is much easier than forming a corporation, because no formal paperwork is required.

A limited liability company (LLC), on the other hand, does offer limited personal liability, like a corporation. And while formal paperwork is required to form an LLC -- also like a corporation -- running an LLC is less complicated. LLC owners do not have to hold regular ownership and management meetings or follow other corporate formalities.

In addition, corporations differ from other business structures in the way they are taxed. The corporation itself must pay corporate income taxes on profits -- that is, whatever is left over after paying salaries, bonuses and other deductible expenses.

In contrast, partnerships, sole proprietorships and LLCs are not taxed on business profits; instead, the profits "pass through" the business to the owners, who report business income or losses on their personal tax returns.

How do I form a corporation?

There are several steps required to legally create a corporation. The first is filing a short document called "articles of incorporation" with the corporations division of your state government.

(Some states refer to this organizational document as a "certificate of incorporation," "articles of organization," a "certificate of formation" or a "charter.") To file this document, you'll have to pay a filing fee of $100 or so. Articles of incorporation contain:

- The name of your corporation
- The corporation's address

- A "registered agent" (the person to be contacted by any member of the public who needs to speak to someone about the corporation), and
- In some states, the names of the corporation's directors.

When forming your corporation, you must also create "corporate bylaws," a longer document that sets out the rules that govern your corporation, including necessary decision-making procedures and voting rights.

Finally, before you start doing business, you must hold an initial meeting of your board of directors to take care of some formalities, and you need to issue shares of stock to the initial owners (shareholders).

Who should form a corporation?

Because of the expense and formalities involved in setting up a corporation and issuing stock (shares in the corporation), you should form a corporation only if you have good reason to do so.

If you merely want to limit your personal liability for business debts, forming a limited liability company (LLC) is probably smarter, because LLCs are both less expensive to form and less complex to run.

But here are some situations in which incorporating your business instead of forming an LLC may make sense:

- Your business needs the ability to issue stock or stock options to attract key employees or outside investment capital.
- Your business is so profitable that you can save significant income tax dollars by keeping some profits in the corporation each year.

This strategy is called "income splitting" because profits are essentially split between the individual owners and the corporation itself.

- You own a family business and you want to begin making gifts of ownership to your family as part of your financial or estate plan or to plan for the next generation of owners. With a corporation you can easily make gifts of shares in your company without necessarily giving up management control and, if it's done correctly, without paying gift tax.

- Others insist that you incorporate your business. For example, if you are an independent contractor, companies you want to work for may ask you to incorporate before they will sign contracts for your services. This is because if you form a corporation, the IRS is more likely to view you as an independent contractor than an employee -- a less-risky proposition for those who want to hire you.

Does running a corporation involve a lot more paperwork than running other types of businesses?

Corporations must comply with statutory rules that unincorporated businesses, such as limited liability companies (LLCs), partnerships and sole proprietorships, don't have to bother with. For instance, corporations must observe corporate formalities such as holding (and taking minutes of) annual shareholder and director meetings and documenting important directors' decisions.

Also, corporations must file and pay taxes on a separate corporate tax return and must set up a double-entry bookkeeping system to record business transactions, complete with daily journals and a general ledger.

How is corporate income taxed?

Unlike sole proprietors and owners of partnerships and LLCs, a corporation's owners do not pay individual taxes on all business profits. The owners pay taxes only on profits paid out to them in the form of salaries, bonuses and dividends. (Dividends are portions of profits that large corporations sometimes pay out to shareholders in return for their investment in the company.)

The corporation pays taxes, at special corporate tax rates, on any profits that are left in the company from year to year (called "retained earnings").

Note that this taxation scheme does not apply to "S corporations," which are corporations that have elected partnership-style taxation. (Regular corporations, discussed above, are called "C" corporations.)

If your corporation elects to be taxed as an S corporation, all of the corporation's profits and losses will "pass through" to the owners, who will report them on their individual income tax returns.

Is corporate income taxed twice?

Many people have heard that corporate income is taxed twice: once to the corporation itself and then again a second time when earnings are paid out to the corporation's owners (shareholders).

This is true only for earnings paid out to shareholders in the form o. dividends -- that is, profits paid by large corporations to their shareholders in return for their investment in the company.

In practice, this sort of double taxation seldom occurs in a small corporation. The reason is simple: shareholders rarely pay themselves dividends. Instead, they work for the corporation and pay themselves salaries and bonuses.

Because the corporation can deduct salaries and bonuses as ordinary and necessary business expenses, it doesn't have to pay corporate tax on them. (Dividends, on the other hand, are not a tax-deductible corporate expense, so both the corporation and the shareholder must pay tax.)

As long as you work for your corporation, even in a part-time or consulting capacity, you can take home profits in the form of a salary and bonuses, avoiding double taxation.

What is a professional corporation?

A professional corporation is a special kind of corporation that only members of certain professions, such as lawyers, doctors and other healthcare workers, can create. By forming a professional corporation, professionals can limit their personal liability for the malpractice of their associates.

Do I need to worry about securities laws when I issue stock in my corporation?

Securities laws are meant to protect investors from unscrupulous business owners. These laws require corporations to jump through some hoops before accepting investments in exchange for shares of stock (the "securities").

Technically, a corporation is required to register the sale of shares with the federal Securities and Exchange Commission (SEC) and its state securities agency before granting stock to the initial corporate owners (shareholders). Registration takes time and typically involves extra legal and accounting fees.

Fortunately, many small corporations get to skip the registration process because of exemptions provided by both federal and state laws. For example, SEC rules don't require a corporation to register a "private offering," which is a non-advertised sale of stock to either:

- A limited number of people (generally 35 or fewer), or
- Those who, because of their net worth or income earning capacity, can reasonably be expected to take care of themselves in the investment process.

Most states have enacted their own versions of this popular federal exemption.

If you and a few associates are setting up a corporation that you'll actively manage, you will no doubt qualify for an exemption, and you will not have to file any paperwork. For more information about federal exemptions, visit the SEC website.

Limited Liability Company FAQ

What is a limited liability company?

A limited liability company, commonly called an "LLC," is a business structure that fits somewhere between the partnership or sole proprietorship and the corporation. Like owners of partnerships or sole proprietorships, LLC owners report business profits or losses on their personal income tax returns; the LLC itself is not a separate taxable entity.

Like a corporation, however, all LLC owners are protected from personal liability for business debts and claims -- a feature known as "limited liability." This means that if the business owes money or faces a lawsuit for some other reason, only the assets of the business itself are at risk.

Creditors normally can't reach the personal assets of the LLC owners, such as a house or car. (Both LLC owners and corporate shareholders can lose this protection by acting illegally, unethically or irresponsibly.)

For these reasons, many people say the LLC combines the best features of both the partnership and corporate business structures.

How many people do I need to form an LLC?

You can be the sole owner of your LLC (limited liability company) in all states except Massachusetts, which is expected to allow the formation of one-person LLCs in the future. Until it does, married business owners in Massachusetts can form an LLC with their spouse to satisfy the current two-owner requirement.

Who should form an LLC?

You should consider forming an LLC (limited liability company) if you are concerned about personal exposure to lawsuits arising from your business. **For example**, if you decide to open a store-front business that deals directly with the public, you may worry that your commercial liability insurance won't fully protect your personal assets from potential slip-and-fall lawsuits or claims by your suppliers for unpaid bills.

Running your business as an LLC may help you sleep better, because it instantly gives you personal protection against these and other potential claims against your business.

Not all businesses can operate as LLCs, however. Businesses in the banking, trust and insurance industry, for example, are typically prohibited from forming LLCs.

In addition, some states, including California, prohibit professionals such as architects, accountants, doctors and other licensed healthcare workers from forming LLCs.

How do I form an LLC?

In most states, the only legal requirement is that you file "articles of organization" with your state's LLC filing office, which is usually part of the Secretary of State's office. (A few states refer to this organizational document as a "certificate of organization" or a "certificate of formation.")

Most states provide a fill-in-the-blank form that takes just a few minutes to prepare. You can obtain the form by mail or download it from your state's website (check your state's Secretary of State or corporations division home page).

A few states require an additional step: Prior to filing your articles of organization, you must publish your intention to form an LLC in a local newspaper.

You'll also want to prepare an LLC operating agreement, though it isn't legally required in most states. Your operating agreement explicitly states the rights and responsibilities of the LLC owners.

The main reasons to do this are to clarify your business arrangements, and to vary from the requirements of your state's LLC laws. If you don't create a written operating agreement, the LLC laws of your state will govern your LLC.

Do I need a lawyer to form an LLC?
Yes/No. All states allow business owners to form their own LLC by filing articles of organization. In most states, the information required for the articles of organization is non-technical -- it typically includes the name of the LLC, the location of its principal office, the names and addresses of the

LLC's owners and the name and address of the LLC's registered agent (a person or company that agrees to accept legal papers on behalf of the LLC).

Now that most states provide downloadable fill-in-the-blank form and instructions, the process is even easier. And LLC filing offices are becoming more accustomed to dealing directly with business owners; they often allow business owners to email questions to them directly.

Of course, if you're trying to decide whether the LLC is the right structure for your business, you may want to consult an expert. You may also want an expert to review your operating agreement or set up your bookkeeping and accounting systems.

Must every LLC have an operating agreement?

Although most states' LLC laws don't require a written operating agreement, you shouldn't consider starting business without one. Here's why an operating agreement is necessary:
• It helps to ensure that courts will respect your personal liability protection by showing that you have been conscientious about organizing your LLC.
• It sets out rules that govern how profits will be split up, how major business decisions will be made, and the procedures for handling the departure and addition of members.
• It helps to avert misunderstandings between the owners over finances and management.
• It keeps your LLC from being governed by the default rules in your state's LLC laws, which might not be to your benefit.

How are LLCs taxed?

Like sole proprietorships (one-owner businesses) and partnerships, an LLC is not a considered separate from its owners for tax purposes. This means that the LLC does not generally pay any income taxes itself; instead, the LLC owners pay taxes on their allocated share of profits (or deduct their share of business losses) on their personal tax returns.

LLC owners can instead elect to have their LLC taxed like a corporation. This may reduce taxes for LLC owners who will regularly need to retain a significant amount of profits in the company.

How do LLCs operate?

Informally. Unlike corporations, LLCs are allowed to operate without holding regular ownership and management meetings. You can hold formal meetings that are documented by written minutes whenever you wish, but doing so is normally voluntary under state LLC laws.

You may wish to call a meeting only when you want to create a paper trail of an important LLC decision, such as the admission or expulsion of a member or the approval of a sizable loan or purchase of real estate.

What are the differences between a limited liability company and a partnership?

The main difference between an LLC and a partnership is that LLC owners are not personally liable for the company's debts and liabilities. This means that creditors of the LLC usually cannot go after the owners' personal assets to pay off LLC debts.

Partners, on the other hand, do not receive this limited liability protection unless they are designated "limited" partners in their partnership agreement.

Also, owners of limited liability companies must file formal articles of organization with their state's LLC filing office, pay a filing fee and comply with certain other state filing requirements before they open for business.

By contrast, people who form a partnership don't need to file any formal paperwork and don't have to pay any special fees.

LLCs and partnerships are almost identical when it comes to taxation, however. In both types of businesses, the owners report business income or losses on their personal tax returns; the business itself does not pay tax on this money.

In fact, LLC and partnerships file the same informational tax return with the IRS (Form 1065) and distribute the same schedules to the business's owners (Schedule K-1, which lists each owner's share of income).

Can I convert my existing business to an LLC?

Yes. Converting a sole proprietorship or a partnership to an LLC is an easy way for sole proprietors and partners to protect their personal assets without changing the way their business income is taxed.

Some states provide a simple form for converting a partnership to an LLC (often called a "certificate of conversion"). Sole proprietors and partners in states that don't provide a conversion form must file regular articles of organization to create an LLC.

In some states, before a partnership can officially convert to an LLC, it must publish a notice in a local newspaper that the partnership is being terminated. And in all states, you'll have to transfer all identification numbers, licenses and permits to the name of your new LLC, including:

- Your federal employer identification number
- Your state employer identification number
- Your sales tax permit
- Your business license (or tax registration), and
- Any professional licenses or permits.

Do I need to know about securities laws to set up an LLC?

If you'll be the sole owner of your LLC and you don't plan to take investments from outsiders, your ownership interest in the LLC will not be considered a "security" and you don't have to concern yourself with these laws. For co-owned LLCs, however, the answer to this question is not so clear.

First, let's consider the definition of a "security." A security is an investment in a profit-making enterprise that is not run by the investor. Here's another way to think about it: If a person invests in a business with the expectation of making money from the efforts of *others*, that person's investment is generally considered a "security" under federal and state law.

Conversely, when a person will rely on his or her own efforts to make a profit (that is, he or she will be an active owner of an LLC), that person's ownership interest in the company will not usually be treated as a security.

How does this apply to you? Generally, if all of the owners will actively manage the LLC -- the situation for most small start-up LLCs -- the LLC ownership interests will not be considered securities.

But if one or more of your co-owners will not work for the company or play an active role in managing the company -- as may be true for LLCs that accept investments from friends and family or that are run by a special management group -- your LLC's ownership interests may be treated as securities by your state and by the federal Securities and Exchange Commission (SEC).

If your ownership interests are considered securities, you must get an exemption from the state and federal securities laws before the initial owners of your LLC invest their money. If you don't qualify for an exemption to the securities laws, you must register the sale of your LLC's ownership interests with the SEC and your state.

Fortunately, smaller LLCs, even those that plan to sell memberships to passive investors, usually qualify for securities law exemptions.

For example, SEC rules exempt the private sale of securities if all owners reside in one state and all sales are made within the state; this is called the "intrastate offering" exemption. Another federal exemption covers "private offerings."

A private offering is an unadvertised sale that is limited to a small number of people (35 or fewer) or to those who, because of their net worth or income earning capacity, can reasonably be expected to be able to take care of themselves in the investment process.

Most states have enacted their own versions of these popular federal exemptions.

Nonprofit Corporations FAQ

What is a nonprofit corporation?
A nonprofit corporation is a corporation formed to carry out a charitable, educational, educational, religious, literary or scientific purpose. A nonprofit corporation doesn't pay federal or state income taxes on profits it makes from activities in which it engages to carry out its objectives.

This is because the IRS and state tax agencies believe that the benefits the public derives from these organizations' activities entitle them to a special tax-exempt status.

The most common federal tax exemption for nonprofits comes from Section 501(c)(3) of the Internal Revenue Code, which is why nonprofits are sometimes called 501(c)(3) corporations.

What are the benefits of forming a nonprofit corporation?

Nonprofit corporations enjoy an exemption from corporate income taxes on profits from activities that are related to their organizational purpose.

Also, a nonprofit is permitted to raise funds by receiving public and private grant money and donations from individuals and companies. (And the tax laws encourage people and businesses to donate money and property by allowing donors to deduct their contributions on their own tax returns.)

Finally, structuring an organization as a nonprofit corporation protects its directors, officers and members from personal liability for the corporation's debts and liabilities.

How do you form a nonprofit corporation?

There are several steps you must take to create a nonprofit corporation. The first is filing a short document, usually called "articles of incorporation," with the corporations division of your state government. To do this, you'll have to pay a filing fee of $30 or so. Articles of incorporation contain:

- The name of your corporation
- The corporation's address
- A "registered agent" (a person who agrees to receive legal papers on behalf of the corporation.)
- The names of the corporation's directors.

After you file your articles, you must apply for state and federal income tax exemptions (the most common federal tax exemption comes from Section 501(c)(3) of the Internal Revenue Code), which require you to complete a fairly lengthy set of forms.

You must also write "corporate bylaws," a document that sets out the rules that govern your corporation, including procedures for making major business decisions, voting rights and other important guidelines. Finally, before you start doing business, you must elect a board of directors and hold an initial meeting of the board.

Is it difficult to run a nonprofit corporation?

Although operating a nonprofit corporation requires some attention to detail, as long as you understand and follow some basic rules, you'll be fine. The first rule is to hold required meetings of directors and members and to keep minutes of these meetings in a corporate records book.

The IRS also has a thing or two to say about what a nonprofit can and cannot do. For instance, a nonprofit cannot make political lobbying a substantial part of its total activities, and a nonprofit must make sure that its activities don't personally benefit its directors, officers or members.

73

So you want to be your own boss!

Maybe you're tired of taking orders from someone who doesn't know as much as you do about your job . . . or tired of fighting rush hour traffic . . . or disgusted with office politics . . . . Perhaps you are convinced you can make more on your own than you can working for someone else -- or you just want to bring in a little extra money to pay for a few luxuries in life -- or your family really needs two incomes but you don't want your kids to be latchkey kids.

Whatever your reason, being your own boss can be personally and financially rewarding--if you come up with the right business idea.

What kind of business idea is the RIGHT idea? Virtually any idea that meets these criteria:

- It is something you know how to do and can do well.

- It is something you LIKE to do and wouldn't mind doing day after day.

- It is something with a broad enough appeal to sell on a steady basis.

- It can be sold at a price that will cover all of your expenses and overhead plus return a healthy profit.

- You have or can raise sufficient funds to get the business started and keep it running until it becomes a profitable venture.

If you haven't yet found your entrepreneurial niche, perhaps you'll spot one or more ideas that sound promising (based on the criteria just mentioned) on the next pages. Some can be started as home based business, others really can't.

Most can be turned into full time businesses, but some are ideal for moonlighting, or as add-on sales in an existing business. All are viable ways to make money, if you know the business and market it properly. Here, then, is the list of business ideas:

Consulting

Agricultural Consultant
Air Quality Consultant
Coach (Personal Or Business)
Computer Consultant
Construction Management Consultant
Diversity Consultant
Engineering Consultant
Environmental Consultant
Expert Witness
Failure Evaluation
Franchise Consultant
Healthcare Consultant
Human Resources

Image Consultant
International Consultant
Marketing Consultant
Medical Office Consultant
Product Development
Proposal (Government Contracts)
Proposal Consultant (Grants)
Retail Consultant
Risk Management
Safety Consultant
Total Quality Management
Training Consultant
Utility Auditing Consultant

Retail and commercial product sales or distributorships

Antique Shop
Used Book Store
Bicycle Sales
Books
Boutique Owner
Calligraphy
Chemicals
Chinese Take-Out Service
Clothing
Coffee Shop Owner
Craft Broker
Craft Supplies Catalog
Fishing Supplies
Gift Baskets

Handmade Soap
Homemade Foods
Janitorial Supplies
Jewelry
Mail Order Business
Pizza Parlor, Posters
Restaurant Owner
Sewing Crafts
Stamps
Tapes
Used Books
Wood Crafts

Sales

Manufacturer's Sales Representative
Multilevel Marketing Or Direct Sales Of Cosmetics, Foods, Telecommunications Services, Etc.
Telemarketing Service
Sales Coach Or Trainer
Advertising Specialties
Direct Selling
Printer Toner Recharging

Planning And Organizing Businesses

Business Plan Writing
Business Turnarounds
Closet Organizing
Event Management

Meeting Planning
Party Planning
Show Promoting
Wedding Planning

Consumer And Business Services

900 Number Businesses (Information Services)
Advertising Agency
Advertising Specialty Sales
Appliance Repair
Audio Tape Duplication
Bed And Breakfast Inn
Bicycle Repair
Bulletin Board Sysop
Business Plan Writer
Business Plan Writing
Cabinet Maker
Car Detailing
Carpet And Upholstery
Catering
Chemical Testing

Chimney Sweep
Cleaning Service (House Ar Building)
Clown
Coin Dealer
Collectibles Dealer
Collections Service
Concrete Construction And Repair
Cook
Cosmetologist
Crafts Instructor
Currency Auctions
Dance Instructor
Daycare For Adults
Daycare For Children

Consumer And Business Services Cont'

Dental Claims Processing
Directory Publishing
Disk Duplication
Electrician
Employment Agency
Environmental Cleanup
Errand Service
Executive Recruiter
Financial Planner
Flea Market Seller
Food Delivery Service
Formal Wear Rental
Framing Service
Genealogist
Grant Writer
Hair Dresser
Handyman Services
Home Automotive Tune-Up
Service
Organizational Services
Housekeeper
Information Broker
Interior Decorating Service
Inventory Control Service
Janitorial Service
Landscaping
Laundry Service
Lawn Cutting
Lawnmower Motor Repair
Limousine Service
Loan Consultant
Locksmith
Magician
Mailing Service
Market Research

Medical Claims Processing
Medical Transcription
Moving Company
Novelty T-Shirt Sales
Painter
Personal Fitness Trainer
Pet Sitting, Pet Walking
Plumber
Pool Cleaning Service

Print Broker
Private Investigator
Public Relations Agency
Public Speaker
Remodeling Service
Screen Printing
Shopping Service
Shuttle Service
Sightseeing Tours
Small Business Consultant
Pool Maintenance
Tax Preparation
Telemarketing Service
Telephone Service Reseller
Tool Rental
Translation Service
Travel Agency
Tutor
TV Repair
VCR Repair
Video Duplication
Wedding Photography
Window Cleaning
Yard Cleanup

Editorial & Graphic Design

Advertising Agency
Advertising Copywriter
Cartoonist
Columnist
Commercial Photographer
Computer Animator
Directory Publisher
Editor
Ghost Writer
Graphic Artist
Index Books
Literary Agent
Multimedia Presentation

Newsletter Production
Nonfiction Writer
Novelist
Proofreader
Publicist
Subscription Newsletter
Translator
Web Designer
Web Content Provider
Write Audio Cassette Scri
Write Book Jacket Blurbs
Write Company Histories
Write Publicity Releases

Office Services

Desktop Publishing
Bookkeeping
Commercial Art
Legal Transcription
Legal Transcription

Mailing List Management
Medical Claims Processin
Medical Transcription
Resume Writing
Word Processing

Computer Businesses

Computer Consulting
Computer Repair
Computer Disk Back Up Services

Computer Programming
Computer Training
Web Site Development
Web Site Hosting

Entertainment

Agent
Ballet Studio
Band Leader
Dance Company

Dancer
One-Man Band
Singer
Song Writer

Miscellaneous Services

Environmental Restoration
Fund Raiser
Plant Nursery (Raise And Sell House Plants And Annuals)
Raising And Racing Horses

Automotive

Auto Detailing
Auto Parts Sales
Auto Repair Garage
Brake Replacement & Repair
Car Wash
Junk Car Removal
Muffler Shop

CHECKLIST FOR GETTING STARTED IN BUSINESS

1. Decide whether to buy an existing business, start a new business, or buy a franchise
2. Decide on the form of business: general partnership, limited liability company, corporation, limited partnership, or sole proprietorship
3. Prepare a business plan.
4. Estimate how much cash you will need to start your business advertising, fixtures, decorating, inventory, fees, working capital, etc. and estimate your monthly expenses.
5. If the business will be incorporated, select the state of incorporation. (Compare the features of corporation laws, organization fees, and taxes of other states.)
6. If you will form a partnership, draft the partnership agreement
7. Check local ordinances regarding zoning permits, and licenses your business may require.
8. File a business certificate (d/b/a)
9. Determine whether to file for S Corporation status
10. Schedule incorporation to obtain maximum state tax savings.
11. Check federal securities requirements.
12. Check "blue sky" law requirements.
13. Check costs of qualification in foreign states.

14. Obtain a minute book, corporate seal, and stock certificates.
15. Conduct a market analysis to determine the viability of your enterprise.
16. Select and reserve a corporate name (first and second choices).
17. Select officers and directors (names, addresses, and Social Security numbers).
18. Develop marketing, advertising, and public relations plans.
19. Develop a capitalization/borrowing/credit/ debt service plan and cash flow plan.
20. Develop income projections.
21. Adopt corporate bylaws or an LLC Operating Agreement.
22. Develop a reimbursement plan for expenses and time worked b officers and consultants prior to incorporation.
23. Select a date and place for the annual meeting of shareholders/directors.
24. Open a separate business checking account. The bank will requi a certified copy of your business certificate or a copy of your inco poration or LLC filing receipt. Establish banking procedures and check-signing authority. Maintain a reserve for three to six month of expenses.
25. Install a business phone line. Use an answering machine or answering service. Order telephone directory advertising.

26. Mail and e-mail announcements of your business start-up to the media, potential customers, and friends.
27. Obtain free counseling services from SCORE (SBA Service Corp of Retired Executives) or Small Business Development Centers (SBDCs).
28. To prevent workplace violence, implement procedures for employee screening, physical security, incident response teams, and reporting system
29. Obtain and design a Web site for marketing, order taking, and communications
30. Identify all patents, trademarks, service marks, or copyrights yo business will have to register or purchase
31. Retain an attorney
32. If you have to borrow money, review potential sources of collateral and prepare a loan package and business plan.
33. Shop around for the best interest rate and terms on a loan.

34. Find an accountant, preferably a certified public accountant (CPA) familiar with tax requirements, and have him or her set up record keeping, payroll, and tax-withholding accounts Your CPA should help you prepare cash flow and financial statements for your business plan and recommend tax strategies.

35. Obtain all necessary government forms, such as workers' compensation and Immigration and Naturalization Service forms and forms for unemployment insurance.

36. Identify product suppliers, the mechanics of delivery of supplies to your business, delivery time, and risk of loss

37. Lease or buy real estate to house your business.

38. If walk-in trade is important, check vehicular or pedestrian traffic patterns at the site you have selected.

39. Draft necessary employment contracts "Employment Agreement".

40. Prepare covenants forbidding employees and/or consultants from revealing your trade secrets, trade lists, or other confidential information and from competing with you after they leave your employ

41. Prepare an employment application and job descriptions "Is Your Employment Application a Danger Spot?" and "Employment Application" forms.

42. Set up a record keeping system including payroll records

43. Ensure that your will and/or living trust provides for the equity in your business.

44. Draw up a buy-sell agreement for stock.

45. Apply for an employer identification number and state sales tax identification number.

46. Establish credit procedures ("Are Debtors Getting Away with Murder?" and "Application for Credit" form).

47. Establish check-cashing procedures and safeguards

48. Lease or buy equipment ("Lease It and Save!").

49. Establish an employee compensation and benefits package ("Fringe Benefits").

50. Prepare an employee manual ("Beware of Your Employee Manual," and "Employee Manual" form).

51. Decide whether to hire or lease employees, independent contractors, and/or utilize a special service firm for various bookkeeping and payroll functions

52. If you are buying used equipment, check with your state department of taxation to determine whether there are any liens for unpaid sales tax against the equipment; check with the county and state to determine whether there are any Uniform Commercial

Code (UCC) filings or chattel mortgages; and obtain a bill of sale from the seller containing an affidavit that he or she has full right to sell and transfer the equipment and that it is free and clear of any and all liens, mortgages, debts, and other encumbrances or claims of any kind.

53. Have an independent appraiser calculate the replacement value of your property to determine how much insurance you need.

54. Find a competent insurance broker and obtain the following insurance: workers' compensation; disability; liability; fire; business interruption; life; automobile; crime; group health; delayed profits; rental value; and flood. Compare premium prices among agents.

More Funding Information

SBA Loan Programs
The SBA offers numerous loan programs to assist small businesses. It is important to note, however, that the SBA is primarily a guarantor of loans made by private and other institutions.

Basic 7(a) Loan Program

FUNCTION: Serves as the SBA's primary business loan program to help qualified small businesses obtain financing when they might not be eligible for business loans through normal lending channels. It is also the agency's most flexible business loan program, since financing under this program can be guaranteed for a variety of general business purposes.

Loan proceeds can be used for most sound business purposes including working capital, machinery and equipment, furniture and fixtures, land and building (including purchase, renovation and new construction), leasehold improvements, and debt refinancing (under special conditions). Loan maturity is up to 10 years for working capital and generally up to 25 years for fixed assets.

CUSTOMER: Start-up and existing small businesses, commercial lending institutions.
DELIVERED THROUGH: Commercial lending institutions.

Basic 7(a) Loan Program

7(a) loans are the most basic and most used type loan of SBA's business loan programs. Its name comes from section 7(a) of the Small Business Act, which authorizes the Agency to provide business loans to American small businesses.

Lenders who are called participants because they participate with SBA in the 7(a) program provide all 7(a) loans. Not all lenders choose to participate, but most American banks do.

There are also some non-bank lenders who participate with SBA in the 7(a) program, which expands the availability of lenders making loans under SBA guidelines.

7(a) loans are only available on a guaranty basis. This means they are provided by lenders who choose to structure their own loans by SBA's requirements and who apply and receive a guaranty from SBA on a portion of this loan.

The SBA does not fully guaranty 7(a) loans. The lender and SBA share the risk that a borrower will not be able to repay the loan in full. The guaranty is a guaranty against payment default. It does not cover imprudent decisions by the lender or misrepresentation by the borrower.

Under the guaranty concept, commercial lenders make and administer the loans. **The business applies to a lender for their financing.** The lender decides if they will make the loan internally or if the application has some weaknesses, which, in their opinion, will require an SBA, guaranty if the loan is to be made.

The guaranty, which SBA provides, is only available to the lender. It assures the lender that in the event the borrower does not repay their obligation and a payment default occurs, the Government will reimburse the lender for its loss, up to the percentage of SBA's guaranty. Under this program, the borrower remains obligated for the full amount due. All 7(a) loans which SBA guaranty must meet 7(a) criteria.

The business gets a loan from its lender with a 7(a) structure and the lender gets an SBA guaranty on a portion or percentage of this loan. Hence the primary business loan assistance program available to small business from the SBA is called the 7(a) guaranty loan program.

A key concept of the 7(a) guaranty loan program is that the loan actually comes from a commercial lender, not the Government. If the lender is not willing to provide the loan, even if they may be able to get an SBA guaranty, the Agency can not force the lender to change their mind.

Neither can SBA make the loan by itself because the Agency does not have any money to lend. Therefore it is paramount that all applicants positively approach the lender for a loan, and that they know the lenders criteria and requirements as well as those of the SBA. In order to obtain positive consideration for an SBA supported loan, the applicant must be both eligible and creditworthy.

WHAT SBA SEEKS IN A LOAN APPLICATION

In order to get a 7(a) loan, the applicant must first be eligible. Repayment ability from the cash flow of the business is a primary consideration in the SBA loan decision process but good character, management capability, collateral, and owner's equity contribution are also important considerations. All owners of 20 percent or more are required to personally guarantee SBA loans.

ELIGIBILITY CRITERIA

All applicants must be eligible to be considered for a 7(a) loan. The eligibility requirements are designed to be as broad as possible in order that this lending program can accommodate the most diverse variety of small business financing needs.

All businesses that are considered for financing under SBA's 7(a) loan program must: meet SBA size standards, be for-profit, not already have the internal resources (business or personal) to provide the financing, and be able to demonstrate repayment.

Certain variations of SBA's 7(a) loan program may also require additional eligibility criteria. Special purpose programs will identify those additional criteria. Eligibility factors for all 7(a) loans include: size, type of business, use of proceeds, and the availability of funds from other sources.

CHARACTER CONSIDERATIONS:

SBA must determine if the principals of each applicant firm have historically shown the willingness and ability to pay their debts and whether they abided by the laws of their community. The Agency must know if there are any factors which impact on these issues. Therefore, a "Statement of Personal History" is obtained from each principal.

OTHER ASPECTS OF THE BASIC 7(a) LOAN PROGRAM

In addition to credit and eligibility criteria, an applicant should be aware of the general types of terms and conditions they can expect if SBA is involved in the financial assistance. The specific terms of SBA loans are negotiated between an applicant and the participating financial institution, subject to the requirements of SBA. In general, the following provisions apply to all SBA 7(a) loans. However certain Loan Programs or Lender Programs vary from these standards.

SBA offers multiple variations of the basic 7(a) loan program to accommodate targeted needs.

Prequalification Program

FUNCTION: Allows business applicants to have their loan applications for $250,000 or less analyzed and potentially sanctioned by the SBA before they are taken to lenders for consideration. The program focuses on the applicant's character, credit, experience and reliability rather than assets.

An SBA-designated intermediary works with the business owner to review and strengthen the loan application. The review is based on key financial ratios, credit and business history, and the loan-request terms. The program is administered by the SBA s Office of Field Operations and SBA district offices.

CUSTOMER: Designated small businesses.

DELIVERED THROUGH: Nonprofit intermediaries such as small business development centers and certified development companies operating in specific geographic areas.

Prequalification Program

The Prequalification Loan program uses intermediary organization to assist prospective borrowers in developing viable loan application packages and securing loans. This program targets low income borrowers, disabled business owners, new and emerging businesses, veterans, exporters, rural and specialized industries.

The job of the intermediary is to work with the applicant to make sure the business plan is complete and that the application is both eligible and has credit merit. If the intermediary is satisfied that the application has a chance for approval, it will send it to the SBA for processing.

To find out whether there is a pre-qualification intermediary operating in your area, contact your local **SBA office**. Note: Small Business Development Centers serving as intermediaries do not charge a fee for loan packaging. For-profit organizations will charge a fee.

Once the loan package is assembled, it is submitted to the SBA for expedited consideration. SBA conducts a thorough analysis of the case, using the same time frame and degree of analysis that it uses when processing requests under the regular method of delivery process.

If SBA decides the application is eligible and has sufficient credit merit to warrant approval, it will issue a commitment letter on behalf of the applicant. The commitment letter or pre-qualification letter, indicates SBA's willingness to guaranty a loan made by a lender under certain terms and conditions.

The intermediary then helps the borrower locate a lender offering the most competitive rates. The applicant then takes the letter and its application documents to a lender for a decision.

Policies Specific to the Prequalification Program
The maximum loan amount for this pilot program is $250,000. Interest Rates, Maturities, Collateral policy, and Guaranty percentages all follow the standard 7(a) loan program.

Micro-Loans

FUNCTION: Provides short-term loans of up to $35,000 to small businesses and not-for-profit child-care centers for working capital or the purchase of inventory, supplies, furniture, fixtures, machinery and/or equipment. Proceeds cannot be used to pay existing debts or to purchase real estate.

The SBA makes or guarantees a loan to an intermediary, who in turn, makes the micro loan to the applicant. These organizations also provide management and technical assistance. The SBA does not guarantee the loans. The micro loan program is available in selected locations in most states.

CUSTOMER: Small businesses and not-for-profit child-care centers needing small-scale financing and technical assistance for start-up or expansion.

DELIVERED THROUGH: Specially designated intermediary lenders (nonprofit organizations with experience in lending and in technical assistance).

Micro-Loans

The MicroLoan Program provides very small loans to start-up, newly established, or growing small business concerns. Under this program, SBA makes funds available to nonprofit community based lenders (intermediaries), which in turn, make loans to eligible borrowers in amounts up to a maximum of $35,000.

The average loan size is about $10,500. Applications are submitted to the local intermediary and all credit decisions are made on the local level.

TERMS, INTEREST RATES AND FEES:

The maximum term allowed for a microloan is six years. However, loan terms vary according to the size of the loan, the planned use of funds, the requirements of the intermediary lender, and the needs of the small business borrower. Interest rates vary, depending upon the intermediary lender and costs to the intermediary from the U.S. Treasury.

COLLATERAL

Each intermediary lender has its own lending and credit requirements. However, business owners contemplating application for a microloan should be aware that intermediaries will generally require some type of collateral, and the personal guarantee of the business owner.

TECHNICAL ASSISTANCE

Each intermediary is required to provide business based training and technical assistance to its microborrowers. Individuals and small businesses applying for microloan financing may be required to fulfill training and/or planning requirements before a loan application is considered.

PROGRAM: Certified Development Company (CDC), a 504 Loan Program

FUNCTION: Provides long-term, fixed-rate financing to small businesses to acquire real estate or machinery or equipment for expansion or modernization.

Typically a 504 project includes a loan secured from a private-sector lender with a senior lien, a loan secured from a CDC (funded by a 100 percent SBA-guaranteed debenture) with a junior lien covering up to 40 percent of the total cost, and a contribution of at least 10 percent equity from the borrower. The maximum SBA debenture generally is $1 million (and up to $1.3 million in some cases).

Customers: Small businesses requiring-brick and mortar- financing.

DELIVERED THROUGH: Certified development companies (private, nonprofit corporations set up to contribute to the economic development of their communities or regions)

Certified Development Company (504) Loan Program

The CDC/504 loan program is a long-term financing tool for economic development within a community. The 504 Program provides growing businesses with long-term, fixed-rate financing for major fixed assets, such as land and buildings.

A Certified Development Company is a nonprofit corporation set up to contribute to the economic development of its community. CDCs work with the SBA and private sector lenders to provide financing to small businesses. There are about 270 CDCs nationwide. Each CDC covers a specific geographic area.

Typically, a 504 project includes a loan secured with a senior lien from a private-sector lender covering up to 50 percent of the project cost, a loan secured with a junior lien from the CDC (backed by a 100 percent SBA-guaranteed debenture) covering up to 40 percent of the cost, and a contribution of at least 10 percent equity from the small business being helped.

Maximum Debenture
The maximum SBA debenture is $1,000,000 for meeting the job creation criteria or a community development goal. Generally, a business must create or retain one job for every $50,000 provided by the SBA.

The maximum SBA debenture is $1.3 million for meeting a public policy goal. The public policy goals are as follows:
- Business district revitalization
- Expansion of exports
- Expansion of minority business development
- Rural development
- Enhanced economic competition
- Restructuring because of federally mandated standards or policies

- Changes necessitated by federal budget cutbacks
- Expansion of small business concerns owned and controlled by veterans
- Expansion of small business concerns owned and controlled by women

WHAT FUNDS MAY BE USED FOR:

Proceeds from 504 loans must be used for fixed asset projects such as: purchasing land and improvements, including existing buildings, grading, street improvements, utilities, parking lots and landscaping; construction of new facilities, or modernizing, renovating or converting existing facilities; or purchasing long-term machinery and equipment. The 504 Program cannot be used for working capital or inventory, consolidating or repaying debt, or refinancing.

TERMS, INTEREST RATES AND FEES:

Interest rates on 504 loans are pegged to an increment above the current market rate for five-year and 10-year U.S. Treasury issues. Maturities of 10 and 20 years are available. Fees total approximately three (3) percent of the debenture and may be financed with the loan.

COLLATERAL:

Generally, the project assets being financed are used as collateral. Personal guaranties of the principal owners are also required.

ELIGIBLE BUSINESSES:

To be eligible, the business must be operated for profit and fall within the size standards set by the SBA. Under the 504 Program, the business qualifies as small if it does not have a tangible net worth in excess of $7 million and does not have an average net income in excess of $2.5 million after taxes for the preceding two years. Loans cannot be made to businesses engaged in speculation or investment in rental real estate.

Another Capital Alternatives

There are many factors that can create a need for additional capital. Some of the more common are as follows:

1. Sales growth requires inventories to be built to support the higher sales level.
2. Sales growth creates a larger volume of accounts receivable.
3. Growth requires the business to carry larger cash balances in order to meet its current obligations to employees, trade creditors, and others.
4. Expansion opportunities such as a decision to open a new branch, add a new product, or increase capacity.
5. Cost savings opportunities such as equipment purchases that will lower production costs or reduce operating expenses.

6. Opportunities to realize substantial savings by taking advantage of quantity discounts on purchases that will lower production costs or reduce operating expenses.
7. Opportunities to realize substantial savings by taking advantage of quantity discounts on purchases for inventory, or building inventories prior to a supplier's price increase.
8. Seasonal factors, where inventories must be built before the selling season begins and receivables may not be collected until 30 to 60 days after the selling season ends.
9. Current repayment of obligations or debts may require more cash than is immediately available.
10. Local or national economic conditions which cause sales and profit to decline temporarily.
11. Economic difficulties of customers that can cause them to pay more slowly than expected.
12. Failure to retain sufficient earnings in the business.
13. Inattention to asset management may have allowed inventories or accounts receivable to get out of hand.

Combination. Frequently, the cause cannot be entirely attributed to any one of these factors, but results from a combination. For example, a growing, apparently successful business may find that it does not have sufficient cash on hand to meet a current debt installment or to expand to a new location because customers have been slow in paying.

Short- and Long-Term Capital. Capital needs can be classified as either short- or long-term. Short-term needs are generally those of less than one year. Long-term needs are those of more than one year.

Short-Term Financing. Short-term financing is most common for assets that turn over quickly such as accounts receivable or inventories. Seasonal businesses that must build inventories in anticipation of selling requirements and will not collect receivables until after the selling season often need short-term financing for the interim. Contractors with substantial work-in-process inventories often need short-term financing until payment is received. Wholesalers and manufacturers with a major portion of their assets tied up in inventories and/or receivables also require short-term financing in anticipation of payments from customers.

Long-Term financing. Long-term financing is more often associated with the need for fixed assets such as property, manufacturing plants, and equipment where the assets will be used in the business for several years. It is also a practical alternative in many situations where short-term financing requirements recur on a regular basis.

Recurring Needs. A series of short-term needs could often be more realistically viewed as a long-term need. The addition of long-term capital should eliminate the short-term needs and the crises that could occur if capital were not available to meet a short-term need.

Steady Growth. Whenever the need for additional capital grows continually without any significant pattern, as in the case of a company with steady sales and profit from year to year, long-term financing is probably more appropriate.

Internal sources of capital are those generated within the business. External sources of capital are those outside the business such as suppliers, lenders, and investors. For example, a business can generate capital internally by accelerating collection of receivables, disposing of surplus inventories, retaining profit in the business or cutting costs.

Capital can be generated externally by borrowing or locating investors who might be interested in buying a portion of the business. Before seeking external sources of capital from investors or lenders, a business should thoroughly explore all reasonable sources for meeting its capital needs internally. Even if this effort fails to generate all of the needed capital, it can sharply reduce the external financing requirements, resulting in less interest expense, lower repayment obligations, and less sacrifice of control.

With a lower requirement, the business's ability to secure external financing will be improved. Further, the ability to generate maximum capital internally and to control operations will enhance the confidence of outside investors and lenders. With more confidence in the business and its management, lenders and investors will be more willing to commit their capital.

Internal Sources of Capital.   There are three principal sources of internal capital:
1.   Increasing the amount of earnings kept in the business.
2.   Prudent asset management.
3.   Cost control.

<u>Increased Earnings Retention</u>.   Many businesses are able to meet a of their capital needs through earnings retention. Each year, share-holders' dividends or partners' draws are restricted so that the larg est reasonable share of earnings is retained in the business to fi-nance its growth.

As with other internal capital sources, earnings retention not only reduces any external capital requirement, but also affects the busi-ness' ability to secure external capital. Lenders are particularly con-cerned with the rate of earnings retention.

The ability to repay debt obligations normally depends upon the amount of cash generated through operations. If this cash is used excessively to pay dividends or to permit withdrawals by investors the company's ability to meet its debt obligations will be threat-ened.

<u>Asset Management</u>.   Many businesses have non-productive assets that can be liquidated (sold or collected) to provide capital for short-term needs. A vigorous campaign of collecting outstanding receivables, with particular emphasis on amounts long outstanding can often produce significant amounts of capital. Similarly, invento ries can be analyzed and those goods with relatively slow sales ac-tivity or with little hope for future fast movement can be liquidated The liquidation can occur through sales to customers or through sales to wholesale outlets, as required.

Fixed assets can be sold to free cash immediately. For example, a company automobile might be sold and provide cash of $2,000 or $3,000. Owners and employees can be compensated on an actual mileage basis for use of their personal cars on company business. Or if an automobile is needed on a full-time basis, a lease can be arranged so that a vehicle will be available.

Other assets such as loans made by the business to officers or employees, investments in non-related businesses, or prepaid expenses should be analyzed closely. If they are non-productive, they can often be liquidated so that cash is available to meet the immediate needs of the business.

Any of the above steps can be taken to alleviate short-term cash shortages. On a long-term basis, the business can minimize its external capital needs by establishing policies and procedures that will reduce the possibility of cash shortages caused by ineffective asset management.

These policies could include the establishment of more rigorous credit standards, systematic review of outstanding receivables, periodic analysis of slow-moving inventories, and establishment of profitability criteria so that fixed asset investments are most closely controlled.

Cost Reduction . Careful analysis of costs, both before and after the fact, can improve profitability and therefore the amount of earnings available for retention. At the same time, cost control minimizes the need for cash to meet obligations to trade creditors and others.

Before the fact, a business can establish buying controls that require a written purchase order and competitive bids on all purchases above a specified amount. Decisions to hire extra personnel, lease additional space, or incur other additional costs can be reviewed closely before commitments are made.

After the fact, management should review all actual costs carefully. Expenses can be compared with objectives, experience in previous periods, or with other companies in the industry. Whenever apparent excess is identified, the cause of the excess should be closely explored and corrective action taken to prevent its recurrence. Trade credit is credit extended by suppliers. Ordinarily, it is the first source of extra capital that the small business owner turns to when the need arises.

Informal Extensions. Frequently, this is done with no formal planning by the business. Suppliers' invoices are simply allowed to "ride" for another 30 to 60 days. Unfortunately, this can lead to a number of problems. Suppliers may promptly terminate credit and refuse to deliver until the account is settled, thus denying the business access to sorely needed supplies, materials, or inventory.

Or, suppliers might put the business on a C.O.D. basis, requiring that all shipments be fully paid in cash immediately upon receipt. At a time when a business is obviously strapped for cash, this requirement could have the same effect as cutting off deliveries all together.

Planning Advantages. A planned program of trade credit extensions can often help the business secure extra capital that it needs without recourse to lenders or equity investors. This is particularly true whenever the capital need is relatively small or short in duration.

A planned approach should involve the following:
1. Take full advantage of available payment terms. If no cash discount is offered and payment is due on the 30th day, do not make any payments before the 30th day.
2. Whenever possible, negotiate extended payment terms with suppliers. For example, if a supplier's normal payment terms are net 30 days from the receipt of goods, these could be extended to net 30 days from the end of the month. This effectively "buys" an average of 15 extra days.
3. If the business feels that it needs a substantial increase in time, say 60 to 90 days, it should advise suppliers of this need. They will often be willing to accept it, provided that the business is faithful in its adherence to payment at the later date.
4. Consider the effect of cash discounts and delinquency penalties for late payment. Frequently, the added cost of trade credit may be far more expensive than the cost of alternate financing such as a short-term bank loan.
5. Consider the possibility of signing a note for each shipment, promising payment at a specific later date. Such a note, which may or may not be interest-bearing, would give the supplier evidence of your intent to pay and increase the supplier's confidence in your business.

Ready Availability.   Trade credit is often available to businesses on a relatively informal basis without the requirements for application, negotiation, auditing, and legal assistance often necessary with other capital sources.

Usage.   Trade credit *must be used judiciously.* Its easy availability is particularly welcome in brief periods of limited needs. Used imprudently, however, it can lead to curtailment of relations with key suppliers and jeopardize your ability to locate other, competitive suppliers who are willing to extend credit to your business.

Remember, that on the other side of the transaction there is another business that is trying to manage its sources of capital, too!

Debt capital.   Debt is an amount of money borrowed from a creditor. A note, signed by the borrower, agreeing to repay the principal amount borrowed plus interest on some predetermined basis, usually evidences the amount borrowed.

Borrowing Term.   The terms under which money is borrowed may vary widely. Short-term notes can be issued for periods as brief as 10 days to fill an immediate need. Long-term notes can be issued for a period of several years.

Discounted Notes.   In some case, particularly in short-term borrowing, the total amount of interest due over the term of the note is deducted from the principal before the proceeds are issued to the borrower. Such a note is called a discounted note.

Short-term Borrowing.   Short-term borrowing usually requires repayment within 60 to 90 days. Notes are often renewed, in whole or in part, on the due date, provided that the borrower has lived up to the obligations of the original agreement and the business continues to be a favorable lending risk.

Credit Lines.   When a business has established itself as being worthy of short-term credit, and the amount needed fluctuates from time to time, banks will often establish a line of credit with the business. The line of credit is the maximum amount that the business can borrow at any one time. The exact amount borrowed can vary according to the needs of the business but cannot exceed its established credit line.

These arrangements give the business access to its requirements up to the credit limit or line. However, it pays interest only on the actual amount borrowed, not the entire line of credit available to it.

Long -term Debt.   Long-term debt is borrowing for a period greater than one year. This general classification includes "intermediate debt" which is borrowing for periods of one to 10 years.

Repayment Schedules.   When the terms of a debt are negotiated, a payment schedule is established for both interest obligations and principal repayment. The dates on which principal and interest payments are due should be scheduled carefully.

For example, a manufacturer with heavy sales just before Christmas and receivables collections through January might best be able to schedule repayments in February. If a payment were due in October or November, when inventories were high and receivables were climbing, the payment could be crippling.

Mortgage Loan Repayment Schedules.   Principal and interest payments on mortgages usually involve uniform monthly payments that include both principal and interest. Each successive monthly payment reduces the amount of principal outstanding.

Therefore, the amount of interest owed decreases and the portion of the monthly payment applicable to principal increases. In the early years of a mortgage, the portion of the monthly payment applied against the principal is relatively small, but grows with each payment.

Term Loan Payment Schedules.   For term loans, payment of principal and interest is ordinarily scheduled on an annual, semiannual or quarterly basis.

Availability.   Commercial banks are the ordinary source of short-term loans for the small business. For small businesses, borrowed capital for periods greater than 10 years is usually available only on real estate mortgages. Other long-term borrowing usually falls into the "intermediate" classification and is available for periods up to 10 years. Such loans are called "term loans."

Selecting Type and Term. The type and term of the loan should be based on the purpose for which the funds will be used. Your banker or accountant can help you determine what type of loan is best to meet your needs.

Loans may be secured or unsecured. In a secured loan, the borrower pledges certain assets as collateral (security) to protect the lender in case of default on the loan or failure of the business.

If the business defaults on the loan through failure to meet interest obligations or principal repayments, the noteholder (lender) assumes ownership of the collateral. If the business fails, the noteholder claims ownership of those specific assets pledged as collateral before the claims of other creditors are settled.

Typical Collateral. In long-term borrowing, fixed assets such as real estate or equipment are usually pledged as collateral. For short-term borrowing, inventories or accounts receivable are the usual collateral.

Inventory Financing. Inventory financing is most commonly used in automobile and appliance retailing. As each unit is purchased by the retailer, the manufacturer is paid by the lender. The lender is repaid by the retailer when the unit is sold.

Interest is determined separately for each unit, based upon the actual amount originally paid by the lender and the period between the time the money is paid the lender is reimbursed by the retailer.

Accounts Receivable Financing. Basically, accounts receivable financing falls into two categories as follows:

- Assignments. The business pledges, or "assigns" its receivables as collateral for a loan

- Factoring. The borrower sells its accounts receivable to a lender (factor).

Although these arrangements are not loans, in a pure sense, the effect is the same.

<u>Receivables Assignments.</u> When receivables are assigned, the amount of the loan varies according to the volume of receivables outstanding. Normally the lender will advance some specified percentage of the outstanding accounts receivable up to a specific credit limit.

In many industries, accounts receivable financing is considered a sign of weakness. However, it is quite common in others. This is particularly true in the garment industry and in personal finance companies.

When accounts receivable are assigned, the borrower is still responsible for collection. Upon collection of any receivable, the amount borrowed should be repaid. Interest is based upon the amount borrowed and the time between receipt of proceeds by the borrower and repayment.

Factoring Accounts Receivable. When accounts receivable are factored, they are sold to the factor and the borrower has no responsibility for collection. The borrower pays the factor a service charge based upon the amount of each receivable sold. In addition, the borrower pays interest for the period between the sale of the receivable and the date the customer pays the factor

Since the factor is responsible for collection, it will only purchase those receivables for which is has approved credit. When customers must pay invoices directly to a factor, it may create doubts about the company's financial stability and, therefore, its ability to deliver

However, factoring is also common in some industries. For example, high tech companies often factor receivables to finance growth and research and development and consider this a way to outsource part of their accounting activities.

Unsecured Debt. The secured creditor's risk is reduced by the claim against specific assets of the business. In default or liquidation, the secured creditor can take possession of these assets to recover any unpaid amounts due from the business. Holders of unsecured notes do not enjoy the same protection.

If the company defaults on a payment, the unsecured creditor, under normal circumstances, can only re-negotiate the amount due, perhaps by seeking collateral, or force the company to liquidate. In liquidation, the holder of an unsecured note would normally have no rights that are superior to those of any other creditors.

Restriction On business.   When accepting an unsecured note, the lender will often place certain restrictions on the business. A typical restriction might be to prevent the company from incurring any debt with a prior claim on the assets of the business in the event of default or failure.

For example, a term note agreement might prevent a company from financing its receivables or inventories since this would result in a prior claim against the assets of the business in liquidation.

Such restrictions may have no effect on the business' ability to operate. However, in other cases, such restrictions could be severe. For example, a business may have a chance to sell to a major new customer.

The new customer may insist upon 60 day credit terms which will require the business to seek additional external financing. Normally, this financing might be readily available on realistic terms from a factor.

However, the restriction of the unsecured note could prevent the business from taking advantage of this significant opportunity for sales and profit improvement.

Personal Guarantees.   The liability of a corporation's shareholders is generally limited to the assets of the business. Creditors have no normal claim against the personal assets of the stockholders if the business should fail.

Therefore, many lenders, when issuing credit to small corporations, seek the added protection of a personal guarantee by the owner (or owners). This protects the creditors if the business fails, since they retain a claim against the personal assets of the owners to fulfill the debt obligation.

Interest Rates.   The interest rates at which small businesses borrow are often relatively high. Banks and other commercial lending institutions normally reserve their lowest available interest rate, the so-called prime rate, for those low risk situations such as short-term loans for major corporations and public agencies where the chances of default are slim and the costs for collection, credit search, and other administrative tasks are minimal.

Because of the higher risks involved in loaning to small businesses, lenders often seek greater collateral while charging higher interest rates to offset their added costs of credit search and loan administration.

Unlike debt, equity capital is permanently invested in the business. The business has no legal obligation for repayment of the amount invested or for payment of interest for the use of the funds.

Share of Ownership.   The equity investor shares in the ownership of the business and is entitled to participate in any distribution of earnings through dividends, in the case of corporations or drawings in the case of partnerships.

The extent of the equity investor's participation in the distribution of earnings of a corporation depends upon the number of shares held. In a partnership, the equity investor's participation will depend upon the ownership percentage specified in the partnership agreement.

Voting Rights.   The equity investor's ownership interest also carries the right to participate in certain decisions affecting the business.

Legal liability.   The personal liability of equity investors for debts of the business depends upon the legal form of the organization. Basically, the investor who acquires equity in a partnership could be personally liable for debts of the business if the business should fail. In a corporation, the liability of equity investors (shareholders) is limited to the amount of their investment.

In other words, if a partnership should fail, creditors could have a claim against the personal assets of the individual partners. If a corporation should fail, the only claims of creditors would be against any remaining assets of the corporation, not against any personal assets of the shareholders.

Equity Investor's compensation .   The purchaser of an equity interest in a business expects to be compensated for the investment in any of the three following ways:

1. Income from earnings distribution of the business, either as dividends paid to corporate shareholders or as drawings in a partnership.
2. Capital gain realized upon sale of the business.
3. Capital gain realized from selling his or her interest to other partners.

Capital Gains .   Capital gain is the term used to describe any excess of the selling price of an investment over the initial purchase price. For example, if you purchased an equity interest in a business for $5,000 and later sold it for $8,000, you would realize a capital gain of $3,000 ($8,000 - $5,000).

Tax Advantages .   Long-term capital gains are those realized on investments held for a period longer than six months. These gains are subject to federal income tax at a lower tax rate than on ordinary income. Therefore, income tax advantages are often a major reason for the investor's desire to acquire an equity interest.

Earnings Distribution.   The equity investor in a partnership is entitled to a share of all drawings paid out to partners at a percentage established when the interest was purchased (and defined in the partnership agreement).

For example, assume an investor acquired a 20% interest in a partnership. The distribution of earnings to all partners in a given year is $20,000. The holder of the 20% interest would receive $4,000 ($20,000 X 0.20).

Sale (or Liquidation) of business. If a business is sold or liquidated, the equity investor shares in the distribution of the proceeds. As with an earnings distribution, the share of the proceeds in a corporation sale depends upon the number of shares held. In a partnership, each partner's share of the proceeds is based upon the percentages specified in the partnership agreement.

If the proceeds received by the equity investor exceed the original purchase price, this excess is considered a capital gain and taxed accordingly at effective rates more favorable than those for ordinary income.

If the business were liquidated, the assets would be sold and the proceeds would first be used to discharge any outstanding obligations to creditors. The balance of the proceeds, after these obligations had been fulfilled, would be distributed to the equity investors in accordance with their shareholdings or percentages of interest.

Sale of equity Interest. As a business prospers and grows, the value of an equity interest grows with it. Therefore, the equity investor may be able to sell his or her interest at a price higher than the initial acquisition cost.

For example, an equity investor in a corporation may have purchased his or her interest at $10.00 per share. As the business grows, he or she is able to sell the shares at $15.00 per share, realizing a capital gain of $5.00 (15.00 - $10.00) on each share sold.

Capital Gains vs Dividends. In many cases, the equity investor in a small business is primarily interested in capital gains. Aside from the tax advantages described earlier, the equity investor usually realizes that the earnings of the small business are better retained in the business than distributed as dividends or drawings.

Retention of earnings permits the business to grow so that the value of the equity interest increases. The investor can realize a return on the investment through a capital gain derived from selling his or her shares or upon sale of the business.

Public Stock Offerings.   When businesses are first organized, equity capital is usually secured from a combination of sources such as the original owners' personal savings and through solicitations from friends, relatives, or other persons known to have financial capability for such investments.

As the need for equity capital becomes greater, say $50,000 to $200,000, it is customary to seek capital through the services of professional finders, who receive a fee for securing the capital needed.

These professionals normally have access to wealthy individuals, capital management companies, estates, trusts, and others with sufficient capital to make such an investment.

As higher levels of capital need, shares are sold through public offerings. The public offering seeks to attract a large number of investors to purchase stock, in large or small amounts. A market is then created for the stock. Shares purchased by the public, as well as the shares held by the original owners and any subsequent equity investors, can also be sold at the going market price.

These transactions do not have a direct effect on the business' capital position since it does not receive the proceeds from the sale. The equity investor can realize a capital gain by selling shares at prices higher than the original purchase price.

Risks of Equity Investment.   The equity investor assumes substantial risk. Unlike the secured creditor, the equity investor has no specific claim against any assets of the business. In liquidation, all claims of all creditors must be satisfied before any remaining assets become available for distribution to the owners.

Even then, the equity investor's participation in the proceeds is restricted to a share that is proportionate to the number of shares held or the partnership interest. Since the risks of equity investment are so substantial, particularly in the case of small businesses, equity investors expect a considerably higher return than the lender.

A lender might be willing to loan money to a business at an interest rate of 10% or 12% since it has certain legal protections in the event of default or liquidation. The investor of equity capital in the same business might seek a far higher return, perhaps 20%, 50% or even more in order to compensate for the added risk of equity investment.

Note the following key points:

- There are various sources of capital available to the small business owner. Terms, collateral, cost (interest rate and control) vary for each alternative.
- The need for additional capital occurs frequently in many small businesses.
- The ability of the owners to anticipate the need and to match the type of capital with that need will help them secure capital on the most favorable terms.
- Those businesses that are alert to opportunities for internal capital generation will often find that this effort not only minimizes the need for external capital, but also opens the doors of the outside money market to them.
- You can minimize your need for external financing through proper asset management, cost control and retention of earnings.
- Trade credit can be utilized to maintain favorable supplier relations while taking full advantage of the credit that is available to you from this vital and convenient source.
- Various types of loan arrangements were also explored, considering both short- and long-term needs as well as typical requirements for security through pledging of specific assets or the owners' personal guarantees.
- Finally, the equity capital market was included so that you understand what the equity investor expects in return for a commitment of capital and the effect that the equity investor's interest can have on your business.

With this information you should now understand the advantages and disadvantages of various capital sources. This will help you select the source or combination of sources that is most appropriate for your needs.

Business Credit Reporting Companies And Website

Experian
http://www.experian.com/products/intelliscore.html
ClientChecker
http://www.clientchecker.com/business_credit_reports.htm
FDinsight
http://www.fdinsight.com
D& B
http://sbs.dnb.com/mycompanycredit.asp

Write your own patent
Do it Yourself patent application Save Thousands in attorneys fees
www.patentpro.us

Free Patent Information
Litman Law - US Patent Office Toll-Free 1-800-4-Patent (472-8368)
www.litmanlaw.com

Patent Invention
Professional Research & Prototyping of New Inventions.
www.davison54.com

Investors And Venture Capitalist

http://www.sba.gov/hotlist/sbic.html

U.S. Small Business Administration
Investment Division
409 Third St., S.W. (Mail Code: 7050)
Washington, DC 20416 (202) 205-6510 sbic@sba.gov

Now go to the next level.